I0021750

RELATIONAL DATABASES AND DISTRIBUTED SYSTEMS

ISBN: 978-0-244-07448-7

Andreas Sofroniou, 2018 © Copyright

Andreas Sofroniou, 2018 © Copyright

RELATIONAL DATABASES AND DISTRIBUTED SYSTEMS

ISBN: 978-0-244-07448-7

ANDREAS SOFRONIOU

Contents

ANDREAS SOFRONIOU

ANDREAS SOFRONIOU

Logical Collection of Related Data

Database

A database is a logically organised collection of related data, generally accessed by a set of programs known as a Database Management System (DBMS), which oversees the creation and use of the database and controls access to the data.

The organisation of a database obviates the need to duplicate information to meet the various requirements of different groups of users, and ensures that the data always remains consistent. A large database requires extensive storage facilities. In some organisations and services, databases can be accessed over networks from microcomputers or as videotex.

'Relational' databases and hypertext techniques include extensive and complex cross-reference facilities so that information on related items may be retrieved. Many database programs have been designed to run on micro-computers. Some of these contain computer languages that enable users to change the operation of the database to suit their requirements.

For example, a mailing list on a micro-computer constitutes a simple database in which--if the information were available in a structured format--the DBMS could be instructed to print out the addresses of

7

all the people called Smith, or of everyone on the mailing list living in Melbourne, Australia.

Data

Data (computing) is the information that has been prepared, often in a particular format, for a specific purpose. In computing, the term data is used for material distinct from instructions: for example, if a computer multiplies two numbers together, the numbers themselves are the data, operated on by an instruction (to multiply them together).

In a more restricted sense, data may be the information input for a particular program, as opposed to the results or output. A third meaning uses data as a term for information not in the form of words, sounds, or images: such data is usually information that is stored in a highly organized and compact form suitable for data processing.

Analogue computer

An analogue computer is a computer that uses continuously variable (analogue) quantities to represent numbers. A voltage between 0 and 1 volt might represent numbers between 0.0 and 100.0, for example. Analogue computers can perform complex arithmetical operations extremely quickly with very few components, but they are not very accurate.

8

Digital computers

Digital computers have replaced them almost entirely except in signal processing, where the basic analogue computing elements are still used very widely. Recent work suggests that analogue computing techniques might have a significant future in neural network computers.

Neural network

The neural network is a densely interconnected network of simple computer processing units (neurons) imitating some qualities of the biological nervous system. Unlike traditional computers, neural networks share out the computation simultaneously between many processors (parallel processing), enormously increasing their collective power.

Consequently, neural networks are well-suited to the computationally intensive tasks of artificial intelligence, for example automatic speech recognition and image processing. The behaviour of a neural network is determined by the strength of its interconnections (synapses); large numbers of synapses help the network to recognize patterns in the presence of noise, and enable it to keep working after some of its synapses have been removed.

9

Hypertext

Hypertext is a generic term for computer systems used to store, retrieve, and view multi-dimensional documents. Hypertext systems are more flexible than conventional databases. Links may be made between parts of a hypertext document so that it can be read in a non-standard order, when pursuing a particular topic. Viewed text may be selected by using a mouse or keyboard, and displayed in a window. The first practical hypertext systems were developed in the 1980s, and are particularly suited to multimedia applications.

Data processing

Data processing entails the use of a computer to manipulate data, particularly the routine tasks undertaken in large organizations. For example, the maintenance, retrieval, and analysis of financial records is faster and easier with the aid of computers.

The amount of data which needs to be processed is frequently considerable. Therefore, the data is often organized in the form of a single database. The database is stored on hard disks, magnetic drums, or magnetic tapes attached to computers of substantial power. Large data-processing facilities are often distributed over networks in which a user anywhere on the network can access data anywhere else on the network.

Powerful systems

Expert system

An expert system utilises a set of computer programs that attempts to replicate the expertise and decision-making abilities of a human expert.

Expert systems are the most widely developed area of artificial intelligence, with a variety of applications ranging from medical diagnosis through to financial decision-making and geological prospecting.

They often use a heuristic or self-learning approach to the solution of a problem, in which feedback of the results of a particular course of action influences subsequent decisions.

They usually have two principal parts: a knowledge base (a special database, which contains facts and other information representing the rules and experience of an expert practitioner in a particular field); and an inference engine, which interprets the knowledge base in relation to the particular problem being presented.

Knowledge engineering is the discipline concerned with building expert systems.

11

Fifth-generation computer

A fifth-generation computer is a term applied to computer systems currently being developed specifically to support artificial intelligence.

In the early 1980s Japan set up a major research project intended to develop the computer hardware and software necessary to perform complex tasks such as machine translation of natural languages, speech recognition, and vision in robotics. Similar projects were also started in the USA and Europe.

The use of artificial intelligence to solve practical problems requires very powerful computers and fifth-generation computers are likely to use more complex computer architectures than conventional computers, involving parallel processing. In 1991 Japan began a new ten-year research initiative, replacing the fifth-generation programme, to investigate neural networks.

Artificial intelligence

Artificial intelligence (AI) is based on the principle that 'the science of making machines do things that would require intelligence if done by humans' as defined in 1968 by Marvin Minsky of the Massachusetts Institute of Technology, USA.

Sensing, reasoning, pattern recognition, speech recognition, and problem-solving are among such tasks. The degree of sophistication that constitutes AI tends to be revised upwards with each new generation of computers. At its most ambitious level AI has the goal of creating computers and robots capable of reproducing a broad range of human behaviour. Doubts remain, however, about whether such systems are theoretically or practically possible, because of the vast complexity of the human brain.

Unlike the human brain, most computers act serially, one operation at a time. Even supercomputers developed in the 1980s that use 'parallel processing' to carry out billions of operations per second barely begin to match human brain capacity.

Moreover, it has been argued that the brain does not operate using computable algorithms. Experiments in machine translation of natural languages in the 1960s revealed the 'frame problem': most human thought processes use huge amounts of background knowledge or 'context' which it is very difficult to duplicate in a computer.

However, one important result of AI research is the development of systems known as neural networks, which can be 'taught' to solve problems. These show promise for a number of different AI applications, particularly those involving pattern recognition.

The demands of AI have also stimulated the development of computer languages, such as PROLOG and LISP, which are better suited to represent and process symbolic structures than more conventional languages.

13

'Pseudo-intelligence' is one term for computer applications being developed in translation systems, semi-automatic offices in which human speech and instructions are turned into a properly laid-out document, in linguistic and psycholinguistic studies, and in robotics--replacing human actions by those of a robot, on the production line or in an artificial limb, for example.

Robot sensing is used in weapons guidance systems and in product quality control. The impact of such developments is likely to be huge.

Most approaches to AI require powerful computer hardware, and it is only since the early 1980s that this has become sufficiently cost-effective to make practical applications possible. Fifth-generation computers are being developed specifically for use in artificial intelligence. Expert systems were amongst the first AI techniques to be used in practical applications.

Cybernetics

Cybernetics (from the Greek, *kubernetes*, steersman) refers to the study of communication and control systems in machines, animals, and organizations. The discipline developed immediately after World War II, when control-systems and systems-engineering techniques were applied successfully to certain neurological problems.

The term cybernetics was first applied in English by Wiener.

Cybernetics is characterized by a concentration on the flow of information (rather than energy or material) within a system, and on the use of feedback or 'goal-directed activity' in both technological artefacts and living organisms.

Major areas of cybernetic study have been biological control systems, automation, animal communication, and artificial intelligence (AI).

The recent rapid expansion of AI as a subject area, together with the development of knowledge-based systems and neural networks, have renewed interest in the general cybernetic approach, although the term 'cybernetics' itself is now rarely used.

15

Information retrieval

Accessing details

Information retrieval refers to the use of computers to access information stored electronically. Digital computers were originally developed to perform calculations and process data.

Early systems were slow and had limited storage capacity, but with advances in technology, especially the development of fast, high-capacity magnetic disks, computers began to be used to store as well as process data. For many applications there are significant advantages over traditional paper-based storage.

A computer, running suitable retrieval software, can search vast quantities of data and recover information very rapidly.

For example, many databases containing medical, financial, or legal information are available on-line (directly under the control of the central processor) via computer networks or modems over telephone lines.

With the continuing reduction in the cost of storage, and particularly the development of compact discs, information retrieval is likely to become an increasingly important use for computers.

16

Input device

Input device (computing) is a peripheral which allows information from an external source to be fed into a computer system.

The standard input device for most modern computer systems is a keyboard, similar to a typewriter's but with additional keys which provide a larger range of characters and control functions. Many computers are also equipped with a mouse.

Before the advent of interactive systems, computers used punched card or paper-tape readers as their standard input devices.

Many different input devices are available for more specialist applications. Scanners, digitizers, or even video cameras are used for graphics systems. Point-of-sale terminals may have bar-code readers.

Optical character recognition systems are used in banking, to read codes printed on cheques, or in desk-top publishing systems to convert printed documents into ASCII codes so that they can be stored and processed digitally

17

Database Management System (DBMS)

Search and retrieval

This is the system used for a quick search and retrieval of information from a database. The DBMS determines how data are stored and retrieved.

It must address problems such as security, accuracy, consistency among different records, response time, and memory requirements. These issues are most significant for database systems on computer networks.

Ever-higher processing speeds are required for efficient database management. Relational DBMSs, in which data are organized into a series of tables ("relations") that are easily reorganized for accessing data in different ways, are the most widely used today.

Electronic database

Database *also called electronic database* refers *to* any collection of data, or information that is specially organized for rapid search and retrieval by a computer. Databases are structured to facilitate the storage, retrieval, modification, and deletion of data in conjunction with various data-processing operations. A database management system (DBMS) extracts information from the database in response to queries.

A database is stored as a file or a set of files on magnetic disk or tape, optical disk, or some other secondary storage device. The information in these files may be broken down into records, each of which consists of one or more fields.

Fields are the basic units of data storage and each field typically contains information pertaining to one aspect or attribute of the entity described by the database.

Records are also organized into tables that include information about relationships between its various fields. Although database is applied loosely to any collection of information in computer files, a database in the strict sense provides cross-referencing capabilities.

Using keywords and various sorting commands, users can rapidly search, rearrange, group, and select the fields in many records to retrieve or create reports on particular aggregates of data.

Database records and files must be organized to allow retrieval of the information. Queries are the main way users retrieve database information. The power of a DBMS comes from its ability to define new relationships from the basic ones given by the tables and to use them to get responses to queries.

Typically, the user provides a string of characters, and the computer searches the database for a corresponding sequence and provides the source materials in which those characters appear; a user can request, for example, all records in which the contents of the field for a person's last name is the word Smith.

The many users of a large database must be able to manipulate the information within it quickly at any given time. Moreover, large business and other organizations tend to build up many independent files containing related and even overlapping data, and their data-processing activities often require the linking of data from several files.

Several different types of DBMS have been developed to support these requirements: flat, hierarchical, network, relational, and object-oriented.

Early systems were arranged sequentially (i.e., alphabetically, numerically, or chronologically); the development of direct-access storage devices made possible random access to data via indexes. In flat databases, records are organized according to a simple list of entities; many simple databases for personal computers are flat in structure.

The records in hierarchical databases are organized in a treelike structure, with each level of records branching off into a set of smaller categories.

Unlike hierarchical databases, which provide single links between sets of records at different levels, network databases create multiple linkages between sets by placing links, or pointers, to one set of records in another; the speed and versatility of network

20

databases have led to their wide use within businesses and in e-commerce.

Relational databases

Relational databases are used where associations between files or records cannot be expressed by links; a simple flat list becomes one row of a table, or "relation," and multiple relations can be mathematically associated to yield desired information. Various iterations of SQL (Structured Query Language) are widely employed in DBMS for relational databases.

Object-oriented database

Object-oriented databases store and manipulate more complex data structures, called "objects," which are organised into hierarchical classes that may inherit properties from classes higher in the chain; this database structure is the most flexible and adaptable.

Natural-language text

The information in many databases consists of natural-language texts of documents; number-oriented databases primarily contain information such as statistics, tables, financial data, and raw scientific and technical data. Small databases can be maintained on personal-computer systems and may be used by individuals at home.

21

These and larger databases have become increasingly important in business life, in part because they are now commonly designed to be integrated with other office software, including spreadsheet programs.

Commercial database applications

Typical commercial database applications include airline reservations, production management functions, medical records in hospitals, and legal records of insurance companies.

The largest databases are usually maintained by governmental agencies, business organizations, and universities. These databases may contain texts of such materials as abstracts, reports, legal statutes, wire services, newspapers and journals, encyclopaedias, and catalogues of various kinds.

Reference database

Reference databases contain bibliographies or indexes that serve as guides to the location of information in books, periodicals, and other published literature. Thousands of these publicly accessible databases now exist, covering topics ranging from law, medicine, and engineering to news and current events, games, classified advertisements, and instructional courses.

22

Data warehouse

Increasingly, formerly separate databases are being combined electronically into larger collections known as data warehouses.

Businesses and government agencies then employ "data mining" software to analyse multiple aspects of the data for various patterns. For example, a government agency might flag for human investigation a company or individual that purchased a suspicious quantity of certain equipment or materials, even though the purchases were spread around the country or through various subsidiaries.

Relational database

This is the type of database in which all data are represented in tabular form. The description of a particular entity is provided by the set of its attribute values, stored as one row or record of the table, called a tuple. Similar items from different records can appear in a table column.

The relational approach supports queries that involve several tables by providing automatic links across tables. Payroll data, for example, can be stored in one table and personnel benefits data in another; complete information on an employee can be obtained by joining the tables on employee identification number.

23

In more powerful relational data models, entries can be programs, text, unstructured data in the form of binary large objects (BLOBs), or any other format the user requires.

The relational approach is currently the most popular model for database management system and object-oriented programming.

Object-oriented programming

The object-oriented programming method refers to the use of predefined programming modular units (objects, classes, subclasses, and so forth) in order to make programming faster and easier to maintain.

Object-oriented languages help to manage complexity in large programs. Objects package data and the operations on them so that only the operations are publicly accessible and internal details of the data structures are hidden.

This information hiding made large-scale programming easier by allowing a programmer to think about each part of the program in isolation.

In addition, objects may be derived from more general ones, "inheriting" their capabilities. Such an object hierarchy made it possible to define specialized objects without repeating all that is in the more general ones.

Java

Object-oriented programming began with the Simula language (1967), which added information hiding to ALGOL. Another influential object-oriented language was Smalltalk (1980), in which a program was a set of objects that interacted by sending messages to one another. Since the 1990s, Java has been one of the most successful object-oriented languages.

Systems programming

This refers to the development of computer software that is part of a computer operating system or other control program, especially as used in computer networks. Systems programming covers data and program management, including operating systems, control programs, network software, and database management systems.

Software

These are the instructions that tell a computer what to do. Software comprises the entire set of programs, procedures, and routines associated with the operation of a computer system.

The term was coined to differentiate these instructions from hardware—*i.e.,* the physical components of a computer system. A set of instructions that directs a computer's hardware to perform a task is called a program, or software program.

The two main types of software are system software and application software. System software controls a computer's internal functioning, chiefly through an operating system (*q.v.*), and also controls such peripherals as monitors, printers, and storage devices.

Application software, by contrast, directs the computer to execute commands given by the user and may be said to include any program that processes data for a user.

Application software thus includes word processors, spreadsheets, database management, inventory and payroll programs, and many other "applications." A third software category is that of network software, which coordinates communication between the computers linked in a network.

Software is typically stored on an external long-term memory device, such as a hard drive or magnetic diskette. When the program is in use, the computer reads it from the storage device and temporarily places the instructions in random access memory (RAM). The process of storing and then performing the instructions is called "running," or "executing," a program.

By contrast, software programs and procedures that are permanently stored in a computer's memory using a read-only (ROM) technology are called firmware, or "hard software."

Operating system (OS)

Resources management

This is the program that manages computer's resources, especially the allocation of those resources among other programs. Typical resources include the central processing unit (CPU), computer memory, file storage, input/output (I/O) devices, and network connections.

Management tasks include scheduling resource use to avoid conflicts and interference between programs. Unlike most programs, which complete a task and terminate, an operating system runs indefinitely and terminates only when the computer is turned off.

Modern multiprocessing operating systems allow many processes to be active, where each process is a "thread" of computation being used to execute a program. One form of multiprocessing is called time-sharing, which lets many users share computer access by rapidly switching between them.

Time-sharing must guard against interference between users' programs, and most systems use virtual memory, in which the memory, or "address space," used by a program may reside in secondary memory (such as on a magnetic hard disk drive) when not in

27

immediate use, to be swapped back to occupy the faster main computer memory on demand.

This virtual memory both increases the address space available to a program and helps to prevent programs from interfering with each other, but it requires careful control by the operating system and a set of allocation tables to keep track of memory use.

Perhaps the most delicate and critical task for a modern operating system is allocation of the CPU; each process is allowed to use the CPU for a limited time, which may be a fraction of a second, and then must give up control and become suspended until its next turn. Switching between processes must itself use the CPU while protecting all data of the processes.

Lack of operating systems

The first digital computers had no operating systems. They ran one program at a time, which had command of all system resources, and a human operator would provide any special resources needed.

The first operating systems were developed in the mid-1950s. These were small "supervisor programs" that provided basic I/O operations (such as controlling punch card readers and printers) and kept accounts of CPU usage for billing.

Supervisor programs also provided multiprogramming capabilities to enable several programs to run at once.

This was particularly important so that these early multimillion-dollar machines would not be idle during slow I/O operations.

Powerful operating systems

Computers acquired more powerful operating systems in the 1960s with the emergence of time-sharing, which required a system to manage multiple users sharing CPU time and terminals.

Two early time-sharing systems were CTSS (Compatible Time Sharing System), developed at the Massachusetts Institute of Technology and the Dartmouth College Basic System, and developed at Dartmouth College.

Other multi-programmed systems included Atlas, at the University of Manchester, England, and IBM's OS/360, probably the most complex software package of the 1960s. After 1972 the Multics system for General Electric Co.'s GE 645 computer (and later for Honeywell Inc.'s computers) became the most sophisticated system, with most of the multi-programming and time-sharing capabilities that later became standard.

The minicomputers of the 1970s had limited memory and required smaller operating systems. The most important operating system of that period was UNIX, developed by AT&T for large minicomputers as a simpler alternative to Multics.

29

It became widely used in the 1980s, in part because it was free to universities and in part because it was designed with a set of tools that were powerful in the hands of skilled programmers.

More recently, Linux, an open-source version of UNIX developed in part by a group led by Finnish computer science student Linus Torvalds and in part by a group led by American computer programmer Richard Stallman, has become popular on personal computers as well as on larger "mainframe" computers.

In addition to such general-purpose systems, special-purpose operating systems run on small computers that control assembly lines, aircraft, and even home appliances. They are real-time systems, designed to provide rapid response to sensors and to use their inputs to control machinery.

From the standpoint of a user or an application program, an operating system provides services. Some of these are simple user commands like "dir"—show the files on a disk—while others are low-level "system calls" that a graphics program might use to display an image.

In either case the operating system provides appropriate access to its objects, the tables of disk locations in one case and the routines to transfer data to the screen in the other.

Some of its routines, those that manage the CPU and memory, are generally accessible only to other portions of the operating system.

Contemporary operating systems for personal computers commonly provide a graphical user interface (GUI). The GUI may be an intrinsic part of the system, as in the older Apple Inc.'s Mac OS and Microsoft Corporation's Windows OS; in others it is a set of programs that depend on an underlying system, as in the X Window system for UNIX and Apple's Mac OS X.

Operating systems also provide network services and file-sharing capabilities—even the ability to share resources between systems of different types, such as Windows and UNIX. Such sharing has become feasible through the introduction of network protocols (communication rules) such as the Internet's TCP/IP.

Networking

Computer network

This entails the networking of two or more computers that are connected with one another for the purpose of communicating data electronically.

Besides physically connecting computer and communication devices, a network system serves the important function of establishing a cohesive architecture that allows a variety of equipment types to transfer information in a near-seamless fashion.

Two popular architectures are ISO Open Systems Interconnection (OSI) and IBM's Systems Network Architecture (SNA).

Two basic network types are local-area networks (LANs) and wide-area (or long-haul) networks. LANs connect computers and peripheral devices in a limited physical area, such as a business office, laboratory, or college campus, by means of permanent links (wires, cables, fibre optics) that transmit data rapidly.

A typical LAN consists of two or more personal computers, printers, and high-capacity disk-storage devices called file servers, which enable each computer on the network to access a common set of files.

LAN operating system software, which interprets input and instructs networked devices, allows users to communicate with each other; share the printers and storage equipment; and simultaneously access centrally located processors, data, or programs (instruction sets).

LAN users may also access other LANs or tap into wide-area networks.

LANs with similar architectures are linked by "bridges," which act as transfer points. LANs with different architectures are linked by "gateways," which convert data as it passes between systems.

Wide-area networks connect computers and smaller networks to larger networks over greater geographic areas, including different continents.

They may link the computers by means of cables, optical fibres, or satellites, but their users commonly access the networks via a modem (a device that allows computers to communicate over telephone lines).

The largest wide-area network is the Internet, a collection of networks and gateways linking millions of computer users on every continent.

Relational Database Management

Oracle Corporation

[Formerly, Software Development Laboratories (1977–79), Relational Software Inc. (1979–82), and Oracle Systems Corporation (1982–95)]

Oracle is the global corporation that develops and markets computer software applications for business. The company is best known for its Oracle database software, a relational database management system, and for computer systems and software, such as Solaris and Java, acquired in its purchase of Sun Microsystems in 2010. Oracle is based in Redwood Shores, California.

The company, initially called Software Development Laboratories, was founded in 1977 by Lawrence (Larry) Ellison and Robert (Bob) Miner, computer programmers at the American electronics company Ampex Corporation, and by Edward (Ed) Oates, Ellison's supervisor at Ampex.

Inspired by a research paper written by British-born computer scientist Edgar F. Codd that outlined a relational database model, Ellison and his colleagues saw commercial potential in the approach, which organized large amounts of data in a way that allowed for efficient storage and quick retrieval. The trio set to

34

work developing and marketing a program based on Codd's data management theory.

In 1979 the company released Oracle, the earliest commercial relational database program to use Structured Query Language (SQL), and the versatile database program quickly became popular. Its first customer was the U.S. Air Force, which used the program at Wright-Patterson Air Force Base, near Dayton, Ohio.

Known for innovation and aggressive marketing, the company, renamed Oracle in 1982 after its flagship product, grew rapidly throughout the 1980s, going public in 1986. In 1987 Oracle became the largest database management company in the world.

Although Oracle's eponymous database has seen steady growth, much of Oracle's growth has come through its aggressive acquisitions of software companies with products for a range of business and technology applications. In its history Oracle lays claim to buying more than 50 companies, including high-profile multibillion-dollar purchases of PeopleSoft, Siebel, BEA, and Sun Microsystems.

Disappointing earnings in the early 1990s led to a period of restructuring, and the company faced increasing competition in the database technology market. The company also stumbled in the mid-1990s with its investment in and vocal support for the Network Computer (NC). The NC was not as fully

35

equipped as a standard personal computer and relied on computer servers for its data and software.

Larry Ellison, now Oracle's chief executive officer (CEO), and partners such as Sun Microsystems' Scott McNealy bet that business users of computers would adopt NCs, which would slow the growth and influence of arch-competitor Microsoft Corporation. That ploy failed, and personal computers running the Microsoft Windows operating system continued to dominate business users' desktops.

Ellison met with more success with his early embrace of the Internet. Oracle developed products that were compatible with World Wide Web technologies, which helped the company to grow along with its acquisitions.

Oracle remained a leader in database technology, with versions available for many different operating systems and for a variety of computers ranging from large mainframes to microcomputers. With the acquisition of Sun Microsystems, Oracle acquired not only the computer programming language Java and the operating system Solaris but also the popular open-source database MySQL, which Sun had acquired in 2008 for $1 billion.

The European Union, before it approved the purchase in January 2010, required assurances from Oracle that it would continue to develop and support MySQL.

Types of database models

File systems of varying degrees of sophistication satisfied the need for information storage and processing for several years.

However, large enterprises tended to build many independent files containing related and even overlapping data, and data-processing activities frequently required the linking of data from several files. It was natural, then, to design data structures and database management systems that supported the automatic linkage of files.

Three database models were developed to support the linkage of records of different types.

These are:

(1) The hierarchical model, in which record types are linked in a treelike structure (e.g., employee records might be grouped under a record describing the departments in which employees work);

(2) The network model, in which arbitrary linkages of record types may be created (e.g., employee records might be linked on one hand to employees' departments and on the other hand to their supervisors—that is, other employees); and

(3) The relational model, in which all data are represented in simple tabular form.

37

In the relational model, the description of a particular entity is provided by the set of its attribute values, stored as one row of the table, or relation. This linkage of n attribute values to provide a meaningful description of a real-world entity or a relationship among such entities forms a mathematical n-tuple; in database terminology, it is simply called a tuple.

The relational approach also supports queries (requests for information) that involve several tables by providing automatic linkage across tables by means of a "join" operation that combines records with identical values of common attributes.

Payroll data, for example, could be stored in one table and personnel benefits data in another; complete information on an employee could be obtained by joining the tables on the employee's identification number.

To support any of these database structures, a large piece of software known as a database management system (DBMS) is required to handle the storage and retrieval of data (via the file management system, since the data are physically stored as files on magnetic disk) and to provide the user with commands to query and update the database.

The relational approach is currently the most popular, as older hierarchical data management systems, such as IMS, the information management system produced by IBM, are being replaced by relational database management systems such as IBM's large mainframe

38

system DB2 or the Oracle Corporation's DBMS, which runs on large servers. Relational DBMS software is also available for workstations and personal computers.

The need for more powerful and flexible data models to support non-business applications (e.g., scientific or engineering applications) has led to extended relational data models in which table entries need not be simple values but can be programs, text, unstructured data in the form of binary large objects (BLOBs), or any other format the user requires.

Another development has been the incorporation of the object concept that has become significant in programming languages. In object-oriented databases, all data are objects. Objects may be linked together by an "is-part-of" relationship to represent larger, composite objects. Data describing a truck, for instance, may be stored as a composite of a particular engine, chassis, drive train, and so forth.

Classes of objects may form a hierarchy in which individual objects may inherit properties from objects farther up in the hierarchy. For example, objects of the class "motorized vehicle" all have an engine; members of subclasses such as "truck" or "airplane" will then also have an engine.

Furthermore, engines are also data objects, and the engine attribute of a particular vehicle will be a link to a specific engine object.

39

Multimedia databases, in which voice, music, and video are stored along with the traditional textual information, are becoming increasingly important and also are providing an impetus toward viewing data as objects, as are databases of pictorial images such as photographs or maps. The future of database technology is generally perceived to be a merging of the relational and object-oriented views.

Data integrity

Integrity is a major database issue. In general, integrity refers to maintaining the correctness and consistency of the data. Some integrity checking is made possible by specifying the data type of an item.

For example, if an identification number is specified to be nine digits, the DBMS may reject an update attempting to assign a value with more or fewer digits or one including an alphabetic character.

Another type of integrity, known as referential integrity, requires that an entity referenced by the data for some other entity must itself exist in the database.

For example, if an airline reservation is requested for a particular flight number, then the flight referenced by that number must actually exist.

Although one could imagine integrity constraints that limit the values of data items to specified ranges (to prevent the famous "computer errors" of the type in which a $10 check is accidentally issued as $10,000), most database management systems do not support such constraints but leave them to the domain of the application program.

Access to a database by multiple simultaneous users requires that the DBMS include a concurrency control mechanism to maintain the consistency of the data in spite of the possibility that a user may interfere with the updates attempted by another user.

For example, two travel agents may try to book the last seat on a plane at more or less the same time. Without concurrency control, both may think they have succeeded, while only one booking is actually entered into the database.

A key concept in studying concurrency control and the maintenance of database correctness is the transaction, defined as a sequence of operations on the data that transform the database from one consistent state into another.

To illustrate the importance of this concept, consider the simple example of an electronic transfer of funds (say $5) from bank account A to account B. The operation that deducts $5 from account A leaves the database inconsistent in that the total over all accounts is $5 short.

Similarly, the operation that adds $5 to account B in itself makes the total $5 too much. Combining these two operations, however, yields a valid transaction. The key to maintaining database correctness is

41

therefore to ensure that only complete transactions are applied to the data and that multiple concurrent transactions are executed (under a concurrency control mechanism) in such a way that a serial order can be defined that would produce the same results.

A transaction-oriented control mechanism for database access becomes difficult in the case of so-called long transactions—for example, when several engineers are working, perhaps over the course of several days, on a product design that may not reach a consistent state until the project is complete. The best approach to handling long transactions is a current area of database research.

Databases may be distributed, in the sense that data reside at different host computers on a network. Distributed data may or may not be replicated, but in any case the concurrency-control problem is magnified. Distributed databases must have a distributed database management system to provide overall control of queries and updates in a manner that ideally does not require that the user know the location of the data.

The attainment of the ideal situation, in which various databases fall under the unified control of a distributed DBMS, has been slowed both by technical problems and by such practical problems as heterogeneous hardware and software and database owners who desire local autonomy.

42

Increasing mention is being made of more loosely linked collections of data, known by such names as multi-databases or federated databases.

A closely related concept is interoperability, meaning the ability of the user of one member of a group of disparate systems (all having the same functionality) to work with any of the systems of the group with equal ease and via the same interface.

In the case of database management systems, interoperability means the ability of users to formulate queries to any one of a group of independent, autonomous database management systems using the same language, to be provided with a unified view of the contents of all the individual databases, to formulate queries that may require fetching data via more than one of the systems, and to be able to update data stored under any member of the group.

Many of the problems of distributed databases are the problems of distributed systems in general. Thus distributed databases may be designed as client-server systems, with middleware easing the heterogeneity problems.

Database security

Security is another important database issue. Data residing on a computer is under threat of being stolen, destroyed, or modified maliciously. This is true whenever the computer is accessible to multiple users

43

but is particularly significant when the computer is accessible over a network.

The first line of defence is to allow access to a computer only to authorized, trusted users and to authenticate those users by a password or similar mechanism. But clever programmers have learned how to evade such mechanisms, designing, for example, so-called computer viruses—programs that replicate themselves and spread among the computers in a network, "infecting" systems and potentially destroying files.

Data can be stolen by devices such as "Trojan horses"—programs that carry out some useful task but contain hidden malicious code—or by simply eavesdropping on network communications.

The need to protect sensitive data (e.g., for national security) has led to extensive research in cryptography and the development of encryption standards for providing a high level of confidence that the data is safe from decoding by even the most powerful computer attacks.

The term *computer theft*, however, usually refers not to theft of information from a computer but rather to theft by use of a computer, typically by modifying data. If a bank's records are not adequately secure, for example, someone could set up a false account and transfer money into it from valid accounts for later withdrawal.

Computer Science Methods

Artificial intelligence

Artificial intelligence (AI) is an area of research that goes back to the very beginnings of computer science.

The idea of building a machine that can perform tasks perceived as requiring human intelligence is an attractive one.

The tasks that have been studied from this point of view include game playing, language translation, natural-language understanding, fault diagnosis, robotics, and supplying expert advice.

Computer graphics

Computer graphics is the field that deals with display and control of images on the computer screen.

Applications may be broken down into four major categories:

(1) design (computer-aided design [CAD] systems), in which the computer is used as a tool in designing objects ranging from automobiles to bridges to computer chips by providing an interactive drawing tool and an interface to simulation and analysis tools for the engineer;

45

(2) fine arts, in which artists use the computer screen as a medium to create images of impressive beauty, cinematographic special effects, animated cartoons, and television commercials;

(3) scientific visualization, in which simulations of scientific events—such as the birth of a star or the development of a tornado—are exhibited pictorially and in motion so as to provide far more insight into the phenomena than would tables of numbers; and

(4) human-computer interfaces.

Graphics-based computer interfaces, which enable users to communicate with the computer by such simple means as pointing to an icon with a handheld device known as a mouse, have allowed millions of ordinary people to control application programs like spreadsheets and word processors.

Graphics technology also supports windows (display boxes) environments on the workstation or personal computer screen, which allow users to work with different applications simultaneously, one in each window.

Graphics also provide realistic interfacing to video games, flight simulators, and other simulations of reality or fantasy.

The term *virtual reality* has been coined to refer to interaction with a computer-simulated virtual world.

A challenge for computer science has been to develop algorithms for manipulating the myriad lines, triangles, and polygons that make up a computer image. In order for realistic on-screen images to be generated, the problems introduced in approximating objects as a set of planar units must be addressed.

Edges of objects are smoothed so that the underlying construction from polygons is not visible, and representations of surfaces are textured. In many applications, still pictures are inadequate, and rapid display of real-time images is required.

Both extremely efficient algorithms and state-of-the-art hardware are needed to accomplish such real-time animation. Technical details of graphics displays are discussed in computer graphics.

Computational methods and numerical analysis

The mathematical methods needed for computations in engineering and the sciences must be transformed from the continuous to the discrete in order to be carried out on a computer.

For example, the computer integration of a function over an interval is accomplished not by applying integral calculus to the function expressed as a formula but rather by approximating the area under the function graph by a sum of geometric areas obtained from evaluating the function at discrete points.

Similarly, the solution of a differential equation is obtained as a sequence of discrete points determined, in simplistic terms, by approximating the true solution curve by a sequence of tangential line segments.

When discredited in this way, many problems can be recast in the form of an equation involving a matrix (a rectangular array of numbers) that is solvable with techniques from linear algebra.

Numerical analysis is the study of such computational methods.

Several factors must be considered when applying numerical methods:

(1) The conditions under which the method yields a solution,

(2) The accuracy of the solution and since many methods are iterative,

(3) Whether the iteration is stable (in the sense of not exhibiting eventual error growth), and

(4) How long (in terms of the number of steps) it will generally take to obtain a solution of the desired accuracy.

The need to study ever-larger systems of equations, combined with the development of large and powerful multiprocessors (supercomputers) that allow many operations to proceed in parallel by assigning them to separate processing elements, has sparked much interest in the design and analysis of parallel

48

computational methods that may be carried out on such parallel machines.

Data structures and algorithms

A major area of study in computer science has been the storage of data for efficient search and retrieval. The main memory of a computer is linear, consisting of a sequence of memory cells that are numbered 0, 1, 2,... in order.

Similarly, the simplest data structure is the one-dimensional, or linear, array, in which array elements are numbered with consecutive integers and array contents may be accessed by the element numbers.

Data items (a list of names, for example) are often stored in arrays, and efficient methods are sought to handle the array data. Search techniques must address, for example, how a particular name is to be found.

One possibility is to examine the contents of each element in turn. If the list is long, it is important to sort the data first—in the case of names, to alphabetize them.

Just as the alphabetizing of names in a telephone book greatly facilitates their retrieval by a user, the sorting of list elements significantly reduces the search time required by a computer algorithm as compared to a search on an unsorted list.

Many algorithms have been developed for sorting data efficiently.

These algorithms have application not only to data structures residing in main memory but even more importantly to the files that constitute information systems and databases.

Although data items are stored consecutively in memory, they may be linked together by pointers (essentially, memory addresses stored with an item to indicate where the "next" item or items in the structure are found) so that the items appear to be stored differently than they actually are.

An example of such a structure is the linked list, in which non-contiguously stored items may be accessed in a pre-specified order by following the pointers from one item in the list to the next.

The list may be circular, with the last item pointing to the first, or may have pointers in both directions to form a doubly linked list. Algorithms have been developed for efficiently manipulating such lists— searching for, inserting, and removing items.

Pointers provide the ability to link data in other ways. Graphs, for example, consist of a set of nodes (items) and linkages between them (known as edges).

Such a graph might represent a set of cities and the highways joining them or the layout of circuit elements and connecting wires on a VLSI chip.

Typical graph algorithms include solutions to traversal problems, such as how to follow the links from node to node (perhaps searching for a node with a particular property) in such a way that each node is visited only once.

A related problem is the determination of the shortest path between two given nodes.

A problem of practical interest in designing any network is to determine how many "broken" links can be tolerated before communications begin to fail.

Similarly, in VLSI chip design it is important to know whether the graph representing a circuit is planar, that is, whether it can be drawn in two dimensions without any links crossing each other.

Impact of Computer Systems

Pervasiveness of computer technology

The pervasiveness of computer technology preceding sections of this book   gives some idea of the pervasiveness of computer technology in society.

Many products used in everyday life now incorporate computer systems: programmable, computer-controlled VCRs in the living room, programmable microwave ovens in the kitchen, programmable thermostats to control heating and cooling systems— the list seems endless.

This section will survey a few of the major areas where computers currently have—or will likely soon have—a major impact on society. As noted below, computer technology not only has solved problems but also has created some, including a certain amount of culture shock as individuals attempt to deal with the new technology.

A major role of computer science has been to alleviate such problems, mainly by making computer systems cheaper, faster, more reliable, and easier to use.

Computers in the workplace

Computers are omnipresent in the workplace. Word processors—computer software packages that simplify the creation and modification of textual documents—have largely replaced the typewriter.

Electronic mail has made it easy to transmit textual messages (possibly containing embedded picture and sound files) worldwide, using computers, cellular telephones, and specially equipped televisions via telephone, satellite, and cable television networks.

Office automation has become the term for linking workstations, printers, database systems, and other tools by means of a local area network (LAN). An eventual goal of office automation has been termed the "paperless office."

Although such changes ultimately make office work much more efficient, they have not been without cost in purchasing and frequently upgrading the necessary hardware and software and in training workers to use the new technology.

Computer-integrated manufacturing (CIM)

This is a relatively new technology arising from the application of many computer science sub-disciplines to support the manufacturing enterprise.

The technology of CIM emphasizes that all aspects of manufacturing should be not only computerized as

53

much as possible but also linked into an integrated whole via a computer communication network. For example, the design engineer's workstation should be linked into the overall system so that design specifications and manufacturing instructions may be sent automatically to the shop floor.

The inventory databases should be linked in as well, so product inventories may be incremented automatically and supply inventories decremented as manufacturing proceeds.

An automated inspection system (or a manual inspection station supplied with online terminal entry) should be linked to a quality-control system that maintains a database of quality information and alerts the manager if quality is deteriorating and possibly even provides a diagnosis as to the source of any problems that arise.

Automatically tracking the flow of products from station to station on the factory floor allows an analysis program to identify bottlenecks and recommend replacement of faulty equipment. In short, CIM has the potential to enable manufacturers to build cheaper, higher quality products and thus improve their competitiveness.

Implementing CIM is initially costly, of course, and progress in carrying out this technology has been slowed not only by its cost but also by the lack of standardized interfaces between the various CIM components and by the slow acceptance of standardized communication protocols to support integration.

Although the ideal of CIM is perhaps just beyond reach at the present time, manufacturers are now able to improve their operations by, for example, linking robot controllers to mainframes for easy and correct downloading of revised robot instructions.

Also available are elaborate software packages that simplify the building of databases for such applications as inventories, personnel statistics, and quality control and that incorporate tools for data analysis and decision support.

Telephone system

Making a telephone call no longer should conjure up visions of operators connecting cables by hand or even of electrical signals causing relays to click into place and effect connections during dialling.

The telephone system now is just a multi-level computer network with software switches in the network nodes to route calls to their destinations.

The main advantage is that calls get through much more quickly and reliably than they did in the past. If one node through which a cross-country call would normally be routed is very busy, an alternative routing can be substituted.

A disadvantage is the potential for dramatic and widespread failures; for example (as has happened), a poorly designed routing and flow-control protocol can cause calls to cycle indefinitely among nodes without reaching their destinations until some drastic action is taken by a system administrator.

Electronic banking

The banking business has been revolutionized by computer technology. Deposits and withdrawals are instantly logged into a customer's account, which is perhaps stored on a remote computer.

Computer-generated monthly statements are unlikely to contain any errors unless they arise during manual entry of check amounts. The technology of electronic funds transfer, supported by computer networking, allows the amount of a grocery bill to be immediately deducted from the customer's bank account and transferred to that of the grocery store. Similarly, networking allows individuals to obtain cash instantly and almost worldwide by simply stepping up to an automated teller machine (ATM) and providing the proper card and personal identification number (popularly known as a PIN).

The downside of this technology is the potential for security problems. Intruders can see packets travelling on a network (e.g., being transported via a satellite link) and can perhaps interpret them (if not carefully encrypted) to obtain confidential information on financial transactions. Network access to personal accounts has the potential to let intruders not only see how much money an individual has but also to transfer some of it elsewhere.

Retail

Computer technology has had a significant impact on retail stores. All but the smallest shops have replaced the old-fashioned cash register with a terminal linked to a computer system.

Some terminals require that the clerk type in the code for the item, but most checkout counters include a bar-code scanner, a device that directly reads into the computer the Universal Product Code (UPC) printed on each package.

Cash-register receipts can then include brief descriptions of the items purchased (by fetching them from the computer database), and the purchase information is also relayed back to the computer to cause an immediate adjustment in the inventory data.

The inventory system can easily alert the manager when the supply of some item drops below a specified threshold. In the case of retail chains linked by networks, the order for a new supply of an item may be automatically generated and sent electronically to the supply warehouse.

57

In a less extensively automated arrangement, the manager can send in the order electronically by a dial-up link to the supplier's computer. These developments have made shopping much more convenient. The checkout process is faster, checkout lines are shorter, and the desired item is more likely to be in stock.

In addition, cash-register receipts contain much more information than a simple list of item prices; many receipts now include discount coupons based on the specific items purchased by the shopper.

If there is a downside, it is the need for shoppers to adjust psychologically to not seeing prices on the packages and to the feeling that perhaps the computer is overcharging (as indeed can happen when advertised sale prices are somehow not entered into the system).

Since the mid-1990s one of the most rapidly growing retail sectors, known as electronic commerce, or e-commerce, involves the use of the Internet and proprietary networks to facilitate business-to-business, consumer, and auction sales of everything imaginable—from computers and electronics to books, recordings, automobiles, and real estate.

Automotive industry

The computer technology has been incorporated into automobiles. Computers are involved (as CAD systems) not only in the design of cars but also in the manufacturing and testing process, perhaps making use of CIM technology.

Today's automobiles include numerous computer chips that analyze sensor data and alert the driver to actual and potential malfunctions. For example, the antilock braking system (ABS) is computer controlled.

Other computers provide warnings of actual and potential malfunctions. Automobile manufacturers are developing safer, "smart" airbags and remote tire-pressure monitors.

Although increased reliability has been achieved by implementing such computerization, a drawback is that only automotive repair shops with a large investment in high-tech interfaces and diagnostic tools for these computerized systems can handle any but the simplest repairs.

Databases and data warehouses

Many information systems are primarily delivery vehicles for data stored in databases. A database is a collection of interrelated data (records) organized so that individual records or groups of records can be retrieved to satisfy various criteria.

Typical examples of databases include employee records and product catalogues. Databases support the operations and management functions of an enterprise.

59

Data warehouses contain the archival data, collected over time, that can be mined for information in order to develop and market new products, serve the existing customers better, or reach out to potential new customers. Anyone who has ever purchased something with a credit card—in person, by mail order, or over the Web—is included within such data collections.

Human resources and procedures

Qualified people are a vital component of any information system. Technical personnel include development and operations managers, business analysts, systems analysts and designers, database administrators, computer programmers, computer security specialists, and computer operators.

In addition, all workers in an organization must be trained to utilize the capabilities of information systems. Billions of people around the world are learning about information systems as they use the Web.

Procedures for using, operating, and maintaining an information system are part of its documentation. For example, procedures need to be established to run a payroll program, including when to run it, who is authorized to run it, and who has access to the output.

Types of information systems

Operational, knowledge and management

Information systems consist of three layers: operational support, support of knowledge work, and management support.

Operational support forms the base of an information system and contains various transaction processing systems for designing, marketing, producing, and delivering products and services. Support of knowledge work forms the middle layer; it contains subsystems for sharing information within an organization.

Management support, forming the top layer, contains subsystems for managing and evaluating an organization's resources and goals.

Information systems support operations, knowledge work, and management in organizations. Functional information systems that support a specific organizational function, such as marketing or production, have been supplanted by cross-functional systems.

Such systems can be more effective in the development and delivery of the firm's products and can be evaluated more closely with respect to the business outcomes.

Operational support and enterprise systems

Transaction processing systems support the operations through which products are designed, marketed, produced, and delivered. In larger organizations, transaction processing is frequently accomplished with large integrated systems known as "enterprise systems."

In this case the information systems that support various functional units—sales and marketing, production, finance, and human resources—are integrated into an enterprise resource planning (ERP) system, the principal kind of enterprise system. ERP systems support the value chain—that is, the entire sequence of activities or processes through which a firm adds value to its products.

For example, an individual or another business may submit a custom order over the Web that automatically initiates "just-in-time" production to the customer's specifications through an approach known as mass customization. This involves sending orders from the customers to the firm's warehouses and perhaps to suppliers to deliver materials just in time for a batched custom production run.

Financial accounts are updated accordingly, and billing is initiated. Along with helping to integrate a firm's own value chain, transaction processing systems can also serve to integrate an organization's overall supply chain. This includes all firms involved in

62

designing, producing, marketing, and delivering the goods and services—from raw materials to the final delivery of the product.

A supply chain management (SCM) system manages the flow of products, data, money, and information throughout the entire supply chain, which starts with the suppliers of raw materials, runs through the intermediate tiers of the processing companies, and ends with the distributors and retailers.

For example, purchasing an item at a major retail store generates more than a cash register receipt; it also automatically sends a restocking order to the appropriate supplier, which in turn may call for orders to the supplier's suppliers.

With an SCM system, suppliers can also access a retailer's inventory database over the Web to schedule efficient and timely deliveries.

The third type of enterprise system, customer relationship management (CRM) supports dealing with the company's customers in marketing, sales, service, and new product development. A CRM system gives a business a unified view of each customer and its dealings with that customer, enabling a consistent and proactive customer relationship.

Many transaction processing systems support electronic commerce over the Internet. Among these are systems for online shopping, banking, and securities trading. Other systems deliver information, educational services, and entertainment on demand.

Yet other systems serve to support the search for products with desired attributes, price discovery (for example, via an auction), and delivery of digital products (for example, software, music, movies, or greeting cards).

A growing array of specialized services and information-based products are offered by various organizations on the Web, as an infrastructure for electronic commerce is emerging on a global scale.

Transaction processing systems accumulate the data in databases and data warehouses that are necessary for the higher-level information systems. Enterprise systems also provide software modules needed to perform many of these higher-level functions.

Support of knowledge work

A large proportion of work in an information society involves manipulating abstract information and knowledge (understood in this context as an organized and comprehensive structure of facts, relationships, theories, and insights) rather than directly processing, manufacturing, or delivering tangible materials. Such work is called knowledge work.

Three general categories of information systems support such knowledge work:

- Professional support systems,
- Collaboration systems, and

- Knowledge management systems.

Professional support systems

Professional support systems offer the facilities needed to perform tasks specific to a given profession. For example, automotive engineers use computer-aided engineering (CAE) software together with virtual reality systems to design and test new models for fuel efficiency, handling, and passenger protection before producing prototypes, and later they use CAE in the design and analysis of physical tests.

Biochemists use specialized three-dimensional modelling software to visualize the molecular structure and probable effect of new drugs before investing in lengthy clinical tests.

Investment bankers often employ financial software to calculate the expected rewards and potential risks of various investment strategies. Indeed, specialized support systems are now available for most professions.

Collaboration systems

The main objectives of collaboration systems are to facilitate communication and teamwork among the members of an organization and across organizations. One type of collaboration system, known as a workflow system, is used to route relevant documents

65

automatically to all appropriate individuals for their contributions.

Pricing and approval of a commercial insurance policy is a process that can benefit from such a system. Another category of collaboration systems allows different individuals to work simultaneously on a shared project.

Known as groupware, such systems accomplish this by allowing controlled shared access, often over an intranet, to the work objects, such as business proposals, new designs, or digital products in progress. The collaborators can be located anywhere in the world: in some multinational companies, work on a project continues 24 hours a day.

Other types of collaboration systems include enhanced e-mail and videoconferencing systems, sometimes with tele-presence using avatars of the participants. Yet another type of collaboration software, known as wiki, enables multiple participants to add and edit content. (Some online encyclopaedias are produced on such platforms.)

Collaboration systems can also be established on social network platforms or virtual life systems. The members of the public, as well as potential customers can be drawn in if desired to enable the co-creation of new products or projection of future outcomes.

Knowledge management systems

Knowledge management systems provide a means to assemble and act on the knowledge accumulated throughout an organization. Such knowledge may include the texts and images contained in patents, design methods, best practices, competitor intelligence, and similar sources, with the elaboration and commentary included.

Placing the organization's documents and communications in an indexed and cross-referenced form enables rich search capabilities. Organizational knowledge is often tacit, rather than explicit, so these systems must also direct users to members of the organization with special expertise.

Management support

A large category of information systems comprises those designed to support the management of an organization. These systems rely on the data obtained by transaction processing systems, as well as on data and information acquired outside the organization (on the Web, for example) and provided by business partners, suppliers, and customers.

Management reporting systems

Information systems support all levels of management, from those in charge of short-term schedules and

67

budgets for small work groups to those concerned with long-term plans and budgets for the entire organization.

Management reporting systems provide routine, detailed, and voluminous information reports specific to each manager's areas of responsibility. These systems are typically used by first-level supervisors.

Generally, such reports focus on past and present activities, rather than projecting future performance. To prevent information overload, reports may be automatically sent only under exceptional circumstances or at the specific request of a manager.

Decision support systems and business intelligence

All information systems support decision making, however indirectly, but decision support systems are expressly designed for this purpose.

As these systems have been developed to analyze massive collections of data, they have also become known as business intelligence applications. The two principal varieties of decision support systems are model-driven and data-driven.

In a model-driven decision support system, a pre-programmed model is applied to a relatively limited data set, such as a sales database for the present quarter.

68

During a typical session, an analyst or sales manager will conduct a dialog with this decision support system by specifying a number of what-if scenarios.

For example, in order to establish a selling price for a new product, the sales manager may use a marketing decision support system.

Such a system contains a model relating various factors—the price of the product, the cost of goods, and the promotion expense in various media—to the projected sales volume over the first five years on the market.

By supplying different product prices to the model, the manager can compare predicted results and select the most profitable selling price.

The primary objective of data-driven business intelligence systems is to analyze large pools of data, accumulated over long periods of time in data warehouses, in a process known as data mining.

Data mining aims to discover significant patterns, such as sequences (buying a new house, followed by a new dinner table), clusters, and correlations (large families and van sales), with which decisions can be made.

Predictive data mining attempts to forecast future outcomes based on the discovered trends. Data-driven decision support systems include a variety of statistical models and may rely on various artificial intelligence techniques, such as expert systems, neural networks, and machine learning.

69

In addition to mining numeric data, text mining is conducted on large aggregates of unstructured data, such as the contents of social media that include social networks, wikis, blogs, and micro-blogs. As used in electronic commerce, for example, text mining helps in finding buying trends, targeting advertisements, and detecting fraud.

An important variety of decision support systems enables a group of decision makers to work together without necessarily being in the same place at the same time. These group decision systems include software tools for brainstorming and reaching consensus.

Another category, geographic information systems, can help analyze and display data by using digitized maps. Such data visualization supports rapid decision making. By looking at a geographic distribution of mortgage loans, for example, one can easily establish a pattern of discrimination.

Executive information systems

Executive information systems make a variety of critical information readily available in a highly summarized and convenient form, typically via a graphical digital dashboard.

Senior managers characteristically employ many informal sources of information, however, so that formal, computerized information systems are only of partial assistance.

70

Nevertheless, this assistance is important for the chief executive officer, senior and executive vice presidents, and the board of directors to monitor the performance of the company, assess the business environment, and develop strategic directions for the future.

In particular, these executives need to compare their organization's performance with that of its competitors and investigate general economic trends in regions or countries.

Often individualized and relying on multiple media formats, executive information systems give their users an opportunity to "drill down" from summary information to increasingly focused details.

Acquiring information systems and services

Information systems are a major corporate asset, with respect both to the benefits they provide and to their high costs.

Therefore, organizations have to plan for the long term when acquiring information systems and services that will support business initiatives. On the basis of long-term corporate plans and the requirements of various individuals from data workers to top management, essential applications are identified and project priorities are set.

For example, certain projects may have to be carried out immediately to satisfy a new government reporting

71

regulation or to interact with a new customer's information system. Other projects may be given a higher priority because of their strategic role or greater expected benefits.

Once the need for a specific information system has been established, the system has to be acquired. This is generally done in the context of the already existing information systems architecture of the firm.

The acquisition of information systems can either involve external sourcing or rely on internal development or modification. With today's highly developed IT industry, companies tend to acquire information systems and services from specialized vendors.

The principal tasks of information systems specialists involve modifying the applications for their employer's needs and integrating the applications to create coherent systems architecture for the firm.

Generally, only smaller applications are developed internally. Certain applications of a more personal nature may be developed where the programming environment supports simple end-user enhancement.

Acquisition from external sources

There are several principal ways to acquire an information system from outside the organization.

Many firms have resorted to the outsourcing of their information systems.

Outsourcing entails transferring the major components of the firm's systems, such as data centres, telecommunications, and software development and maintenance, to a specialized company that provides its services under long-term contracts specifying the service levels. In some cases the outsourcing entails moving the services abroad—i.e., offshoring.

Responsibility for the acquisition of new applications then falls to the outside company. In other cases the company may outsource just the development or maintenance of their information systems, with the outside company being a systems developer.

Cloud computing is increasingly being adopted as a source of information services. It offers on-demand access via the Internet to services furnished by a provider that runs data centres with the necessary software.

The services can be provided at one of three levels: as the infrastructure for running existing applications, as the platform for developing new applications, or as software-as-a-service (SaaS) to be used by the firm over the network. In particular, SaaS has become a cost-effective way to use enterprise systems.

Generally, cloud computing is provided by external vendors, although some firms implement their own private clouds in order to share resources and access them over the network. Scalability and avoidance of capital expenditures are notable advantages of public clouds; the partial loss of control is a drawback.

Companies may choose to acquire an application by leasing a proprietary package from a vendor under a license and having the software customized internally or externally by the vendor or another outside contractor. Enterprise systems are generally leased in this way.

An alternative is to deploy an open-source application, whose program code is free and open for all to modify under a different type of license that enforces the openness of the application in perpetuity.

Generally, the costs of the use of open-source software include the technical support from specialized vendors.

Internal information systems development

Information systems life cycle

When an information system is developed internally by an organization, one of two broad methods is used: life-cycle development or rapid application development (RAD).

The development phase of the life cycle for an information system consists of a feasibility study, system analysis, system design, programming and testing, and installation. Following a period of operation and maintenance, typically 5 to 10 years, an evaluation is made of whether to terminate or upgrade the system.

The same methods are used by software vendors, which need to provide more general, customizable systems. Large organizational systems, such as enterprise systems, are generally developed and maintained through a systematic process, known as a system life cycle, which consists of six stages: feasibility study, system analysis, system design, programming and testing, installation, and operation and maintenance.

The first five stages are system development proper, and the last stage is the long-term exploitation. Following a period of use (with maintenance as needed), the information system may be either phased

ANDREAS SOFRONIOU

out or upgraded. In the case of a major upgrade, the system enters another development life cycle.

The principal objective of a feasibility study is to determine whether the system is desirable on the basis of long-term plans, strategic initiatives, and a cost-benefit analysis. System analysis provides a detailed answer to the question, What will the new system do? The next stage, system design, results in an extensive blueprint for how the new system will be organized.

During the programming and testing stage, the individual software modules of the system are developed, tested, and integrated into a coherent operational system.

Further levels of testing ensure continuing quality control. Installation includes final testing of the system in the work environment and conversion of organizational operations to the new system, integrating it with other systems already in place.

The later stages of development include such implementation activities as training users and modifying the organizational processes in which the system will be used.

Life-cycle development is frequently faulted for its long development times and voluminous documentation requirements—and, in some instances, for its failure in fulfilling the user's requirements at the end of the long development road. Increasingly, life-cycle development is being replaced by RAD.

76

In various RAD methodologies a prototype—a preliminary working version of an application—is built quickly and inexpensively, albeit imperfectly.

This prototype is turned over to the users, their reactions are collected, suggested modifications are incorporated, and successive prototype versions eventually evolve into the complete system.

Formal processes for the collaboration between system developers and users, such as joint applications development (JAD), have been introduced by some firms.

Sometimes RAD and life-cycle development are combined: a prototype is produced to determine user requirements during the initial system analysis stage, after which life-cycle development takes over.

Industrial methods of software production and reuse have been implemented in systems development. Thus, reusable software components are developed, tested, and catalogued to be deployed as parts of future information systems.

A particularly important method of component-based development is the use of Web services, which are software objects that deliver a specific function (such as looking up a customer's order in a database) and can be stitched together into inter-organisational information systems enabling business partners to cooperate.

After an installed system is handed over to its users and operations personnel, it will almost invariably be modified extensively over its useful life in a process known as system maintenance. A large system will typically be used and maintained for some 5 to 10 years or even longer.

Most maintenance is to adjust the system to the organization's changing needs and to new equipment and other software, but inevitably some maintenance involves correcting design errors and exterminating software "bugs" as they are discovered.

Managing information systems

For an organization to use its information services to launch a new initiative, those services have to be part of a well-planned infrastructure of core resources. The specific systems ought to be configured into a coherent architecture to deliver the necessary information services.

Many organizations rely on outside firms—that is, specialised IT companies—to deliver some, or even all, of their information services. If located in-house, the management of information systems can be decentralized to a certain degree to correspond to the organization's overall structure.

78

Information system infrastructure and architecture

A well-designed information system rests on a coherent foundation that supports responsive change—and, thus, the organization's agility—as new business or administrative initiatives arises.

Known as the information system infrastructure, the foundation consists of core telecommunications networks, databases and data warehouses, software, hardware, and procedures managed by various specialists.

With business globalization, an organization's infrastructure often crosses many national boundaries. Establishing and maintaining such a complex infrastructure requires extensive planning and consistent implementation to handle strategic corporate initiatives, transformations, mergers, and acquisitions.

Information system infrastructure should be established in order to create meaningful options for future corporate initiatives.

When organized into a coherent whole, the specific information systems that support operations, management, and knowledge work constitute the system architecture of an organization.

Clearly, an organization's long-term general strategic plans must be considered when designing an information system infrastructure and architecture.

Organisation of information services

Information services of an organization are delivered by an outside firm or by an internal unit. Outsourcing of information services helps with such objectives as cost savings, access to superior personnel, and focusing on core competencies.

An information services unit is typically in charge of an organization's information systems. When the systems are largely outsourced, this unit is of a limited size and concentrates on aligning the systems with the corporate competitive strategy and on supervising the outside company's services.

When information services are provided in-house and centralized, this unit is responsible for planning, acquiring, operating, and maintaining information systems for the entire organization.

In decentralised structures, however, the central unit is responsible only for planning and maintaining the infrastructure, while business and administrative specialists supervise systems and services for their own units. A variety of intermediate organizational forms are possible.

In many organizations, information systems are headed by a chief information officer (CIO). The activities of information services are usually supervised by a steering committee consisting of the executives

80

representing various functional units of the organization.

In the organizations where information systems play a strategic role, boards of directors need to be involved in their governance. A vital responsibility of an information services unit is to ensure uninterrupted service and integrity of the systems and information in the face of many security threats.

Information systems security and control

With the opening of information systems to the global Internet and with their thorough infusion into the operation and management of business and government organizations and into the infrastructure of daily life across the world, security issues have moved to the forefront of concerns about global well-being.

81

Information systems security

Information systems security measures

The first step in creating a secure information system is to:

- Identify threats.

Once potential problems are known, the next step is to:

- Establishing controls that can be taken.

Finally, the third step consists of:

- Audits to discover any breach of security.

Information systems security is responsible for the integrity and safety of system resources and activities.

Most organisations in developed countries are dependent on the secure operation of their information systems. In fact, the very fabric of societies often depends on this security.

Information systems are at the heart of intensive care units and air traffic control systems. Financial institutions could not survive a total failure of their information systems for longer than a day or two.

Electronic funds transfer systems (EFTS) handle immense amounts of money that exist only as electronic signals sent over the networks or as

82

magnetized spots on storage disks. Information systems are vulnerable to a number of threats, which require strict controls such as countermeasures and regular audits to ensure that the system remains secure.

Although instances of computer crime and abuse receive extensive media attention, human error is estimated to cause greater losses in information systems operation.

Disasters such as earthquakes, floods, and fires are the particular concern of disaster recovery planning, which is a part of a corporate business continuity plan.

A contingency scheme is also necessary to cover the failure of servers, tele-communications networks, or software.

Computer crime and abuse

Computer crime—illegal acts in which computers are the primary tool—cost the world economy billions of dollars annually. Computer abuse does not rise to the level of crime, yet it involves unethical use of a computer.

The objectives of the so-called hacking of information systems include vandalism, theft of consumer information, governmental and commercial espionage, sabotage, and cyber war. Some of the more widespread means of computer crime include phishing and planting of mal-ware, such as computer viruses and worms, Trojan horses, and logic bombs.

Phishing involves obtaining a legitimate user's login and other information by subterfuge with messages fraudulently claiming to originate with a legitimate entity, such as a bank or government office.

A successful phishing raid to obtain a user's information may be followed by identity theft, an impersonation of the user to gain access to the user's resources.

Computer viruses are a particularly common form of attack. These are program instructions that are able not only to perform malicious acts but also to insert copies of themselves into other programs and thus spread to other computer systems.

Similar to viruses, worms are complete computer programs that replicate through telecommunications networks. Because of their ability to spread rapidly and widely, viruses and worms can inflict immense damage.

The damage can be in the form of tampering with system operation, theft of large volumes of data (e.g., credit card numbers), or denial of service by overloading systems with a barrage of spurious requests.

In a Trojan horse attack, the malefactor conceals unauthorized instructions within an authorized program. A logic bomb consists of hidden instructions,

84

often introduced with the Trojan horse technique, that stay dormant until a specific event occurs, at which time the instructions are activated.

In one well-known case, in 1985 a programmer at an insurance company in Fort Worth, Texas, placed a logic bomb in his company's human resources system; when he was fired and his name was deleted from the company's employee database, the entire database was erased.

Once a system connected to the Internet is invaded, it may be used to take over many others and organize them into so-called botnets that can launch massive attacks against other systems to steal information or sabotage their operation.

Information systems controls

To ensure secure and efficient operation of information systems, an organization institutes a set of procedures and technological measures called controls. Information systems are safeguarded through a combination of general and application controls.

General controls apply to information system activities throughout an organization. The most important general controls are the measures that control access to computer systems and the information stored there or transmitted over telecommunications networks.

85

General controls include administrative measures that restrict employees' access to only those processes directly relevant to their duties. As a result, these controls limit the damage that any individual employee or employee impersonator can do.

Fault-tolerant computer systems installed in critical environments, such as in hospital information systems or securities marketplaces, are designed to control and isolate problems so that the system can continue to function.

Application controls are specific to a given application and include such measures as validating input data, logging the accesses to the system, regularly archiving copies of various databases, and ensuring that information is disseminated only to authorized users.

Securing information

Controlling access to information systems became profoundly more difficult with the spread of wide area networks (WANs) and, in particular, the Internet. Users, as well as interlopers, may access systems from any unattended computer within an organization or from virtually anywhere over the Internet.

As a security measure, each legitimate user has a unique name and a regularly changed password. Another security measure is to require some form of physical authentication, such as an object (a physical token or a smart card) or a personal characteristic (fingerprint, retinal pattern, hand geometry, or signature).

Many systems combine these types of measures—such as automatic teller machines, which rely on a combination of a personal identification number (PIN) and an identification card. Security measures placed between an organization's internal networks and the Internet are known as firewalls.

A different way to prohibit access to information is via data encryption, which has gained particular importance in electronic commerce. Public key encryption is used widely in such commerce. To ensure confidentiality, only the intended addressee has the private key needed to decrypt messages that have been encrypted with the addressee's public key.

Furthermore, authentication of both parties in an electronic transaction is possible through the digital certificates issued to both parties by a trusted third party and the use of digital signatures—an additional code attached to the message to verify its origin. A type of anti-tampering code can also be attached to a message to detect corruption.

Similar means are available to ensure that parties to an electronic transaction cannot later repudiate their participation. Some messages require additional attributes. For example, electronic cash is a type of message, with encryption used to ensure the purchaser's anonymity, which acts like physical cash.

To continually monitor information systems, intrusion detection systems are used. They detect anomalous events and log the information necessary to produce reports and to establish the source and the nature of the possible intrusion. More active systems also attempt to prevent the intrusion upon detection.

Information systems audit

The effectiveness of an information system's controls is evaluated through an information systems audit. An audit aims to establish whether information systems are safeguarding corporate assets, maintaining the integrity of stored and communicated data, supporting corporate objectives effectively, and operating efficiently.

It is a part of a more general financial audit that verifies an organization's accounting records and financial statements.

Information systems are designed so that every financial transaction can be traced. In other words, an audit trail must exist that can establish where each transaction originated and how it was processed.

Aside from financial audits, operational audits are used to evaluate the effectiveness and efficiency of information systems operations, and technological audits verify that information technologies are appropriately chosen, configured, and implemented.

88

Impacts of information systems

Computerized information systems, particularly since the arrival of the Web and mobile computing, have had a profound effect on organisations, economies, and societies, as well as on individuals whose lives and activities are conducted in these social aggregates.

Organisational impacts of information systems

Several essential organisational capabilities are enhanced by information systems.

These systems provide support for:

- Business operations;
- Individual and group decision making;
- New product development;
- Relationships with customers, suppliers, and partners;
- Pursuit of competitive advantage; and, in some cases,
- Business model itself (e.g., Google).

Information systems bring new options to the way companies interact and compete, the way organizations are structured, and the way workplaces are designed.

In general, use of Web-based information systems can significantly lower the costs of communication among

ANDREAS SOFRONIOU

workers and firms and cost-effectively enhance the coordination of supply chains or webs.

This has led many organizations to concentrate on their core competencies and to outsource other parts of their value chain to specialized companies. The capability to communicate information efficiently within a firm has led to the deployment of flatter organizational structures with fewer hierarchical layers.

Nevertheless, information systems do not uniformly lead to higher profits. Success depends both on the skill with which information systems are deployed and on their use being combined with other resources of the firm, such as relationships with business partners or superior knowledge of the industry.

The use of information systems has enabled new organizational structures. In particular, so-called virtual organizations have emerged that do not rely on physical offices and standard organizational charts.

Two notable forms of virtual organizations are the network organization and the cluster organization. In a network organization, long-term corporate partners supply goods and services to and through a central hub firm. Together, a network of small companies can present the appearance of a large corporation.

Indeed, at the core of such an organization may be nothing more than a single entrepreneur supported by only a few employees. Thus, network organization forms a flexible ecosystem of companies, whose formation and work is organized around Web-based information systems.

In a cluster organization, the principal work units are permanent and temporary teams of individuals with complementary skills.

Team members, who are often widely dispersed around the globe, are greatly assisted in their work by the use of Web resources, corporate intranets, and collaboration systems.

Global virtual teams are able to work around the clock, moving knowledge work electronically "to follow the Sun."

Information systems delivered over mobile platforms have enabled employees to work not just outside the corporate offices but virtually anywhere. "Work is the thing you do, not the place you go to" has become the slogan of the emerging new workplace.

Virtual workplaces include home offices, regional work centres, customers' premises, and mobile offices of people such as insurance adjusters. Employees who work in virtual workplaces outside their company's premises are known as telecommuters.

The role of consumers has changed, empowered by the Web. Instead of being just passive recipients of products, they can actively participate with the producers in the co-creation of value. By coordinating their collective work using information systems,

91

individuals have created such products as open-source software and online encyclopaedias.

The value of virtual worlds and massively multiplayer online games has been created largely by the participants.

The electronic word-of-mouth in the form of reviews and opinions expressed on the Web can make or break products.

In sponsored co-creation, companies attract their customers to generate and evaluate ideas, co-develop new products, and promote the existing goods and services.

Information systems in economics and society

International growth

Along with the global transportation infrastructure, network-based information systems have been a factor in the growth of international business and corporations.

A relationship between the deployment of information systems and higher productivity has been shown in a number of industries when these systems complement other corporate resources.

Electronic commerce has moved many relationships and transactions among companies and individuals to the Internet and the Web, with the resulting expansion of possibilities and efficiencies.

The development of the Web-based ecosystem, accompanied by the low cost of hardware and telecommunications and the availability of open-source software, has led to a flowering of entrepreneurial activity and the emergence to prominence and significant market value of numerous firms based on new business models.

Among the examples are electronic auction firms, search-engine firms, social network platforms, and online game companies.

93

Owing to the vast opportunities for moving work with data, information, and knowledge in electronic form to the most cost-effective venue, a global redistribution of work has been taking place. However, the wide deployment of information systems on Web platforms has not positively affected job markets.

As the use of information systems has become pervasive in advanced economies and societies at large, several societal and ethical issues have moved into the forefront. The most important are issues of individual privacy, property rights, universal access and free speech, information accuracy, and quality of life.

Individual privacy hinges on the right to control one's personal information. While invasion of privacy is generally perceived as an undesirable loss of autonomy, government and business organizations do need to collect data in order to facilitate administration and exploit marketing opportunities.

Electronic commerce presents a particular challenge to privacy, as personal information is routinely collected and disseminated in a largely unregulated manner.

The ownership of and control over the personal profiles, contacts, and communications in social networks are one example of a privacy issue that awaits resolution through a combination of market forces, industry self-regulation, and possibly government regulation. Preventing invasions of privacy is complicated by the lack of an international legal standard.

Intellectual property, such as software, books, music, and movies, is protected, albeit imperfectly, by patents, trade secrets, and copyrights. However, such intangible goods can be easily copied and transmitted electronically over the Web for unlawful reproduction and use.

Combinations of legal statutes and technological safeguards, including anti-piracy encryption and electronic watermarks, are in place, but much of the abuse prevention relies on the ethics of the user. The means of protection themselves, such as patents, play a great role in the information society.

However, the protection of business methods (e.g., Amazon's patenting of one-click ordering) is being questioned, and the global enforcement of intellectual property protection encounters various challenges.

Access to information systems over the Web is necessary for full participation in modern society. In particular, it is desirable to avoid the emergence of digital divides between nations or regions and between social and ethnic groups.

Open access to the Web as a medium for human communication and as a repository for shared knowledge is treasured. Indeed, many people consider free speech a universal human right and the Internet and Web the most widely accessible means to exercise this right.

Yet, legitimate concerns arise about protecting children without resorting to censorship. Technological

95

solutions, such as software that filters out pornography and inappropriate communications, are partially successful.

Of concern to everyone is the accuracy and security of information contained in databases and data warehouses—whether in health and insurance data, credit bureau records, or government files—as misinformation or privileged information released inappropriately can adversely affect personal safety, livelihood, and everyday life.

Individuals must cooperate in reviewing and correcting their files, and organizations must ensure appropriate security, access, and use of such files.

Information systems have affected the quality of personal and working lives. In the workplace, information systems can be deployed to eliminate tedious tasks and give workers greater autonomy, or they can be used to thoughtlessly eliminate jobs and subject the remaining workforce to pervasive electronic surveillance.

Consumers can use the Web for shopping, networking, and entertainment—but at the risk of contending with spam (unsolicited e-mail), interception of credit card numbers, and attack by computer viruses.

Information systems can expand participation of ordinary citizens in government through electronic elections, referendums, and polls and also can provide electronic access to government services and information—permitting, for instance, electronic filing of taxes, direct deposit of government checks, and viewing of current and historical government documents.

More transparent and beneficial government operations are possible by opening the data collected by and about governments to public scrutiny in a searchable and easy-to-use form. With the Web, the public sphere of deliberation and self-organization can expand and give voice to individuals.

However, information systems have also conjured Orwellian images of government surveillance and business intrusion into private lives. It remains for society to harness the power of information systems by strengthening legal, social, and technological means.

Information systems as a field of study

Socio-technical approach

Information systems are a discipline of study that is generally situated in business schools. The essential objective of the discipline is to develop and study the theories, methods, and systems of using information technology to operate and manage organizations.

The discipline employs a socio-technical approach, placing the study of information technology in the context of management, organizations, and society.

The academic study of information systems originated in the 1960s. The scholarly society furthering the development of the discipline is the Association for Information Systems (AIS), which is based in the United States.

Query languages

The uses of databases are manifold. They provide a means of retrieving records or parts of records and performing various calculations before displaying the results. The interface by which such manipulations are specified is called the query language.

Whereas early query languages were originally so complex that interacting with electronic databases could be done only by specially trained individuals, recent interfaces are more user-friendly, allowing casual users to access database information.

The main types of popular query modes are the menu, the "fill-in-the-blank" technique, and the structured query. Particularly suited for novices, the menu requires a person to choose from several alternatives displayed on the video terminal screen.

The fill-in-the-blank technique is one in which the user is prompted to enter key words as search statements. The structured query approach is effective with relational databases.

It has a formal, powerful syntax that is in fact a programming language, and it is able to accommodate logical operators. One implementation of this approach, the Structured Query Language (SQL), has the form:

select [field Fa, Fb, . . . , Fn]

from [database Da, Db, . . . , Dn]

where [field Fa = abc] *and* [field Fb = def].

Structured query languages support database searching and other operations by using commands such as "find," "delete," "print," "sum," and so forth.

The sentence-like structure of an SQL query resembles natural language except that its syntax is limited and

99

fixed. Instead of using an SQL statement, it is possible to represent queries in tabular form.

The technique, referred to as query-by-example (or QBE), displays an empty tabular form and expects the searcher to enter the search specifications into appropriate columns. The program then constructs an SQL-type query from the table and executes it.

The most flexible query language is of course natural language. The use of natural-language sentences in a constrained form to search databases is allowed by some commercial database management software.

These programs parse the syntax of the query; recognize its action words and their synonyms; identify the names of files, records, and fields; and perform the logical operations required.

Experimental systems that accept such natural-language queries in spoken voice have been developed; however, the ability to employ unrestricted natural language to query unstructured information will require further advances in machine understanding of natural language, particularly in techniques of representing the semantic and pragmatic context of ideas.

The prospect of an intelligent conversation between humans and a large store of digitally encoded knowledge is not imminent.

Information searching and retrieval

State-of-the-art approaches to retrieving information employ two generic techniques:

(1) Matching words in the query against the database index (key-word searching) and

(2) Traversing the database with the aid of hypertext or hypermedia links.

Key-word searches can be made either more general or narrower in scope by means of logical operators (e.g., disjunction and conjunction).

Because of the semantic ambiguities involved in free-text indexing, however, the precision of the key-word retrieval technique—that is, the percentage of relevant documents correctly retrieved from a collection—is far from ideal, and various modifications have been introduced to improve it.

In one such enhancement, the search output is sorted by degree of relevance, based on a statistical match between the key words in the query and in the document; in another, the program automatically generates a new query using one or more documents considered relevant by the user. Key-word searching has been the dominant approach to text retrieval since the early 1960s; hypertext has so far been largely confined to personal or corporate information-retrieval applications.

Architecture of a networked information system

The exponential growth of the use of computer networks in the 1990s presages significant changes in systems and techniques of information retrieval.

In a wide-area information service, a number of which began operating at the beginning of the 1990s on the Internet computer network, a user's personal computer or terminal (called a client) can search simultaneously a number of databases maintained on heterogeneous computers (called servers).

The latter are located at different geographic sites, and their databases contain different data types and often use incompatible data formats. The simultaneous, distributed search is possible because clients and servers agree on a standard document addressing scheme and adopt a common communications protocol that accommodates all the data types and formats used by the servers.

Communication with other wide-area services using different protocols is accomplished by routing through so-called gateways capable of protocol translation.

Several representative clients are shown: a "dumb" terminal (i.e., one with no internal processor), a personal computer (PC), a Macintosh (Mac), and a NeXT machine.

They have access to data on the servers sharing a common protocol as well as to data provided by services that require protocol conversion via the gateways. Network news is such a wide-area service, containing hundreds of news groups on a variety of subjects, by which users can read and post messages.

Evolving information-retrieval techniques, exemplified by an experimental interface to the NASA space shuttle reference manual, combine natural language, hyperlinks, and key-word searching.

Other techniques, seeking higher levels of retrieval precision and effectiveness, are studied by researchers involved with artificial intelligence and neural networks.

The next major milestone may be a computer program that traverses the seamless information universe of wide-area electronic networks and continuously filters its contents through profiles of organizational and personal interest: the information robot of the 21st century.

Information display

For humans to perceive and understand information, it must be presented as:

- Print and image on paper;
- Print and image on film or on a video terminal;
- Video in motion pictures, on television broadcasts;

103

- Lectures and conferences;
- Face-to-face encounters.

Except for live encounters and audio information, such displays emanate increasingly from digitally stored data, with the output media being video, print, and sound.

Video

Possibly the most widely used video display device, at least in the industrialized world, is the television set. Designed primarily for video and sound, its image resolution is inadequate for alphanumeric data except in relatively small amounts.

Use of the television set in text-oriented information systems has been limited to menu-oriented applications such as videotex, in which information is selected from hierarchically arranged menus (with the aid of a numeric keyboard attachment) and displayed in fixed frames.

The television, computer, and communications technologies are, however, converging in a high-resolution digital television set capable of receiving alphanumeric, video, and audio signals.

The computer video terminal is today's ubiquitous interface that transforms computer-stored data into analogue form for human viewing.

The two basic apparatuses used are the cathode-ray tube (CRT) and the more recent flat-panel display. In CRT displays an electron gun emits beams of electrons on a phosphorus-coated surface; the beams are deflected, forming visible patterns representative of data. Flat-panel displays use one of four different media for visual representation of data: liquid crystal, light-emitting diodes, plasma panels, and electroluminescence.

Advanced video display systems enable the user to scroll, page, zoom (change the scale of the details of the display image for enhancement), divide the screen into multiple colours and windows (viewing areas), and in some cases even activate commands by touching the screen instead of using the keyboard.

The information capacity of the terminal screen depends on its resolution, which ranges from low (character-addressable) to high (bit-addressable).

High resolution is indispensable for the display of graphic and video data in state-of-the-art workstations, such as those used in engineering or information systems design.

Print

Modern society continues to be dominated by printed information. The convenience and portability of print on paper make it difficult to imagine the paperless world that some have predicted. The generation of paper print has changed considerably, however.

Although manual typesetting is still practiced for artwork, in special situations, and in some developing countries, electronic means of composing pages for subsequent reproduction by photo-duplication and other methods has become commonplace.

Since the 1960s, volume publishing has become an automated process using large computers and high-speed printers to transfer digitally stored data on paper. The appearance of microcomputer-based publishing systems has proved to be another significant advance.

Economical enough to allow even small organizations to become in-house publishers, these so-called desktop publishing systems are able to format text and graphics interactively on a high-resolution video screen with the aid of page-description command languages.

Once a page has been formatted, the entire image is transferred to an electronic printing or photocomposition device.

Printers

Computer printers are commonly divided into two general classes according to the way they produce images on paper: impact and non-impact. In the first type, images are formed by the print mechanism making contact with the paper through an ink-coated ribbon.

The mechanism consists either of print hammers shaped like characters or of a print head containing a row of pins that produce a pattern of dots in the form of characters or other images.

Most non-impact printers form images from a matrix of dots, but they employ different techniques for transferring images to paper.

The most popular type, the laser printer, uses a beam of laser light and a system of optical components to etch images on a photoconductor drum from which they are carried via electrostatic photocopying to paper.

Light-emitting diode (LED) printers resemble laser printers in operation but direct light from energised diodes rather than a laser onto a photoconductive surface.

Ion-deposition printers make use of technology similar to that of photocopiers for producing electrostatic images. Another type of non-impact printer, the ink-jet printer, sprays electrically charged drops of ink onto the print surface.

Microfilm and microfiche

Alphanumeric and image information can be transferred from digital computer storage directly to film.

Reel microfilm and microfiche (a flat sheet of film containing multiple micro-images reduced from the original) were popular methods of document storage and reproduction for several decades. During the 1990s they were largely replaced by optical disc technology.

Voice

In synthetic speech generation, digitally pre-stored sound elements are converted to analogue sound signals and combined to form words and sentences. Digital-to-analogue converters are available as inexpensive boards for microcomputers or as software for larger machines.

Human speech is the most effective natural form of communication, and so applications of this technology are becoming increasingly popular in situations where there are numerous requests for specific information (e.g., time, travel, and entertainment), where there is a need for repetitive instruction, in electronic voice mail (the counterpart of electronic text mail), and in toys.

Dissemination of information

The process of recording information by handwriting was obviously laborious and required the dedication of the likes of Egyptian scribes or monks in monasteries around the world. It was only after mechanical means of reproducing writing were invented that information records could be duplicated more efficiently and economically. The first practical method of reproducing writing mechanically was block printing; it was developed in China during the T'ang dynasty (618–907).

Ideographic text and illustrations were engraved in wooden blocks, inked, and copied on paper. Used to produce books as well as cards, charms, and calendars, block printing spread to Korea and Japan but apparently not to the Islamic or European Christian civilizations. European woodcuts and metal engravings date only to the 14th century.

Printing from movable type was also invented in China (in the mid-11th century AD). There and in the bookmaking industry of Korea, where the method was applied more extensively during the 15th century, the ideographic type was made initially of baked clay and wood and later of metal. The large number of typefaces required for pictographic text composition continued to handicap printing in the Orient until the present time.

The invention of character-oriented printing from movable type (1440–50) is attributed to the German printer Johannes Gutenberg. Within 30 years of his invention, the movable-type printing press was in use throughout Europe. Character-type pieces were metallic and apparently cast from metallic moulds;

paper and vellum (calfskin parchment) were used to carry the impressions.

Gutenberg's technique of assembling individual letters by hand was employed until 1886, when the German-born American printer Ottmar Mergenthaler developed the Linotype, a keyboard-driven device that cast lines of type automatically.

Typesetting speed was further enhanced by the Monotype technique, in which a perforated paper ribbon, punched from a keyboard, was used to operate a type-casting machine.

Mechanical methods of typesetting prevailed until the 1960s. Since that time they have been largely supplanted by the electronic and optical printing techniques described in the previous section.

Unlike the use of movable type for printing text, early graphics were reproduced from wood relief engravings in which the nonprinting portions of the image were cut away. Musical scores, on the other hand, were reproduced from etched stone plates. At the end of the 18th century, the German printer Aloys Senefelder developed lithography, a plano-graphic technique of transferring images from a specially prepared surface of stone.

In offset lithography the image is transferred from zinc or aluminium plates instead of stone, and in photo-engraving such plates are superimposed with film and then etched. The first successful photographic process, the daguerreotype, was developed during the 1830s.

110

The invention of photography, aside from providing a new medium for capturing still images and later video in analogue form, was significant for two other reasons.

First, recorded information (textual and graphic) could be easily reproduced from film, and, second, the image could be enlarged or reduced. Document reproduction from film to film has been relatively unimportant, because both printing and photocopying are cheaper.

The ability to reduce images, however, has led to the development of the microform, the most economical method of disseminating analogue-form information. Another technique of considerable commercial importance for the duplication of paper-based information is photocopying, or dry photography.

Printing is most economical when large numbers of copies are required, but photocopying provides a fast and efficient means of duplicating records in small quantities for personal or local use.

Of the several technologies that are in use, the most popular process, xerography, is based on electrostatics. While the volume of information issued in the form of printed matter continues unabated, the electronic publishing industry has begun to disseminate information in digital form.

The digital optical disc is developing as an increasingly popular means of issuing large bodies of archival information—for example, legislation, court and hospital records, encyclopaedias and other reference

111

works, referral databases, and libraries of computer software.

Full-text databases, each containing digital page images of the complete text of some 400 periodicals stored on CD-ROM, entered the market in 1990. The optical disc provides the mass production technology for publication in machine-readable form.

It offers the prospect of having large libraries of information available in virtually every school and at many professional workstations.

The coupling of computers and digital telecommunications is also changing the modes of information dissemination. High-speed digital satellite communications facilitate electronic printing at remote sites; for example, the world's major newspapers and magazines transmit electronic page copies to different geographic locations for local printing and distribution.

Updates of catalogues, computer software, and archival databases are distributed via e-mail, a method of rapidly forwarding and storing bodies of digital information between remote computers.

Indeed, a large-scale transformation is taking place in modes of formal as well as informal communication.

For more than three centuries, formal communication in the scientific community has relied on the scholarly and professional periodical, widely distributed to tens of thousands of libraries and to tens of millions of individual subscribers.

In 1992 a major international publisher announced that its journals would gradually be available for computer storage in digital form; and in that same year the State University of New York at Buffalo began building a completely electronic, paperless library.

The scholarly article, rather than the journal, is likely to become the basic unit of formal communication in scientific disciplines; digital copies of such an article will be transmitted electronically to subscribers or, more likely, on demand to individuals and organizations who learn of its existence through referral databases and new types of alerting information services.

The Internet already offers instantaneous public access to vast resources of non-commercial information stored in computers around the world.

Similarly, the traditional modes of informal communications—various types of face-to-face encounters such as meetings, conferences, seminars, workshops, and classroom lectures—are being supplemented and in some cases replaced by e-mail, electronic bulletin boards (a technique of broadcasting newsworthy textual and multimedia messages between computer users), and electronic teleconferencing and distributed problem-solving (a method of linking remote persons in real time by voice-and-image communication and special software called "groupware").

These technologies are forging virtual societal networks—communities of geographically dispersed individuals who have common professional or social interests.

114

Operational research

Basic aspects

Operational research started as an application of scientific methods to the management and administration of organized military, governmental, commercial, and industrial processes.

Operations research attempts to provide those who manage organized systems with an objective and quantitative basis for decision; it is normally carried out by teams of scientists and engineers drawn from a variety of disciplines.

Thus, operations research is not a science itself but rather the application of science to the solution of managerial and administrative problems, and it focuses on the performance of organized systems taken as a whole rather than on their parts taken separately.

Usually concerned with systems in which human behaviour plays an important part, operations research differs in this respect from systems engineering, which, using a similar approach, tends to concentrate on systems in which human behaviour is not important.

Operations research was originally concerned with improving the operations of existing systems rather than developing new ones; the converse was true of

115

systems engineering. This difference, however, has been disappearing as both fields have matured.

The subject matter of operations research consists of decisions that control the operations of systems. Hence, it is concerned with how managerial decisions are and should be made, how to acquire and process data and information required to make decisions effectively, how to monitor decisions once they are implemented, and how to organize the decision-making and decision-implementation process.

Extensive use is made of older disciplines such as logic, mathematics, and statistics, as well as more recent scientific developments such as communications theory, decision theory, cybernetics, organization theory, the behavioral sciences, and general systems theory.

In the 19th century the Industrial Revolution involved mechanization or replacement of human by machine as a source of physical work. Study and improvement of such work formed the basis of the field of industrial engineering.

Many contemporary issues are concerned with automation or mechanization of mental work. The primary technologies involved are mechanization of symbol generation (observation by machines such as radar and sonar), mechanization of symbol transmission (communication by telephone, radio, and television), and mechanization of logical manipulation

116

of symbols (data processing and decision making by computer).

Operations research applies the scientific method to the study of mental work and provides the knowledge and understanding required to make effective use of personnel and machines to carry it out.

History of science to management

In a sense, every effort to apply science to management of organised systems, and to their understanding, was a predecessor of operations research. It began as a separate discipline, however, in 1937 in Britain as a result of the initiative of A.P. Rowe, superintendent of the Bawdsey Research Station, who led British scientists to teach military leaders how to use the then newly developed radar to locate enemy aircraft.

By 1939 the Royal Air Force formally commenced efforts to extend the range of radar equipment so as to increase the time between the first warning provided by radar and the attack by enemy aircraft.

At first they analyzed physical equipment and communication networks, but later they examined behaviour of the operating personnel and relevant executives. Results of the studies revealed ways of improving the operators' techniques and also revealed unappreciated limitations in the network.

117

Similar developments took place in the British Army and the Royal Navy, and in both cases radar again was the instigator. In the army, use of operations research had grown out of the initial inability to use radar effectively in controlling the fire of antiaircraft weapons. S

Since the traditional way of testing equipment did not seem to apply to radar gun-sights, scientists found it necessary to test in the field under operating conditions, and the distinguished British physicist and future Nobel Laureate P.M.S. Blackett organized a team to solve the antiaircraft problem. Blackett's Antiaircraft Command Research Group included two physiologists, two mathematical physicists, an astrophysicist, an army officer, a former surveyor, and subsequently a third physiologist, a general physicist, and two mathematicians.

By 1942 formal operations research groups had been established in all three of Britain's military services.

Development of operations research paralleling that in Britain took place in Australia, Canada, France, and, most significantly for future developments, in the United States, which was the beneficiary of a number of contacts with British researchers.

Sir Robert Watson-Watt, who with A.P. Rowe launched the first two operational studies of radar in 1937 and who claims to have given the discipline its name, visited the United States in 1942 and urged that operations research be introduced into the War and

118

Navy departments. Reports of the British work had already been sent from London by American observers, and James B. Conant, then chairman of the National Defence Research Committee, had become aware of operations research during a visit to England in the latter half of 1940.

Another stimulant was Blackett's memorandum, "Scientists at the Operational Level," of December 1941, which was widely circulated in the U.S. service departments.

The first organized operations research activity in the United States began in 1942 in the Naval Ordnance Laboratory. This group, which dealt with mine warfare problems, was later transferred to the Navy Department, from which it designed the aircraft mining blockade of the Inland Sea of Japan.

As in Britain, radar stimulated developments in the U.S. Air Force. In October 1942, all Air Force commands were urged to include operations research groups in their staffs. By the end of World War II there were 26 such groups in the Air Force. In 1943 Gen. George Marshall suggested to all theatre commanders that they form teams to study amphibious and ground operations.

At the end of World War II a number of British operations research workers moved to government and industry. Nationalization of several British industries was an important factor. One of the first industrial groups was established at the National Coal Board.

Electricity and transport, both nationalized industries, began to use operations research shortly thereafter. Parts of the private sector began to follow suit, particularly in those industries with cooperative research associations; for example, in the British Iron and Steel Research Association.

The early development of industrial operations research was cautious, and for some years most industrial groups were quite small. In the late 1950s, largely stimulated by developments in the United States, the development of industrial operations research in Britain was greatly accelerated.

Although in the United States military research increased at the end of the war, and groups were expanded, it was not until the early 1950s that American industry began to take operations research seriously.

The advent of the computer brought an awareness of a host of broad system problems and the potentiality for solving them and within the decade about half the large corporations in the United States began to use operations research. Elsewhere the technique also spread through industry.

Societies were organized, beginning with the Operational Research Club of Britain, formed in 1948, which in 1954 became the Operational Research Society. The Operations Research Society in America was formed in 1952.

Many other national societies appeared; the first international conference on operations research was held at Oxford University in 1957. In 1959 an International Federation of Operational Research Societies was formed.

The first appearance of operations research as an academic discipline came in 1948 when a course in non-military techniques was introduced at the Massachusetts Institute of Technology in Cambridge.

In 1952 a curriculum leading to a master's and doctoral degree was established at the Case Institute of Technology (now Case Western Reserve University) in Cleveland.

Since then many major academic institutions in the United States have introduced programs. In the United Kingdom courses were initiated at the University of Birmingham in the early 1950s. The first chair in operations research was created at the newly formed University of Lancaster in 1964. Similar developments have taken place in most countries in which a national operations research society exists.

The first scholarly journal, the *Operational Research Quarterly*, published in the United Kingdom, was initiated in 1950; in 1978 its name was changed to the *Journal of the Operational Research Society*.

It was followed in 1952 by the *Journal of the Operations Research Society of America*, which was renamed *Operations Research* in 1955. The International Federation of Operational Research Societies initiated

121

the *International Abstracts in Operations Research* in 1961.

Despite its rapid growth, operations research is still a relatively young scientific activity. Its techniques and methods, and the areas to which they are applied, can be expected to continue to expand rapidly. Most of its history lies in the future.

Essential characteristics

Three essential characteristics of operations research are a systems orientation, the use of interdisciplinary teams, and the application of scientific method to the conditions under which the research is conducted.

Systems orientation

The systems approach to problems recognizes that the behaviour of any part of a system has some effect on the behaviour of the system as a whole. Even if the individual components are performing well, however, the system as a whole is not necessarily performing equally well.

For example, assembling the best of each type of automobile part, regardless of make, does not necessarily result in a good automobile or even one that will run, because the parts may not fit together. It is the interaction between parts, and not the actions of any single part, that determines how well a system performs.

Thus, operations research attempts to evaluate the effect of changes in any part of a system on the performance of the system as a whole and to search for causes of a problem that arises in one part of a system in other parts or in the interrelationships between parts. In industry, a production problem may be approached by a change in marketing policy.

For example, if a factory fabricates a few profitable products in large quantities and many less profitable items in small quantities, long efficient production runs of high-volume, high-profit items may have to be interrupted for short runs of low-volume, low-profit items.

An operations researcher might propose reducing the sales of the less profitable items and increasing those of the profitable items by placing salesmen on an incentive system that especially compensates them for selling particular items.

Inter-disciplinary team

Scientific and technological disciplines have proliferated rapidly in the last 100 years. The proliferation, resulting from the enormous increase in scientific knowledge, has provided science with a filing system that permits a systematic classification of knowledge.

123

This classification system is helpful in solving many problems by identifying the proper discipline to appeal to for a solution.

Difficulties arise when more complex problems, such as those arising in large organized systems, are encountered. It is then necessary to find a means of bringing together diverse disciplinary points of view.

Furthermore, since methods differ among disciplines, the use of interdisciplinary teams makes available a much larger arsenal of research techniques and tools than would otherwise be available. Hence, operations research may be characterized by rather unusual combinations of disciplines on research teams and by the use of varied research procedures.

Methodology

Until the 20th century, laboratory experiments were the principal and almost the only method of conducting scientific research. But large systems such as are studied in operations research cannot be brought into laboratories.

Furthermore, even if systems could be brought into the laboratory, what would be learned would not necessarily apply to their behaviour in their natural environment, as shown by early experience with radar.

Experiments on systems and subsystems conducted in their natural environment ("operational experiments") are possible as a result of the experimental methods developed by the British statistician R.A. Fisher in 1923–24. For practical or even ethical reasons, however, it is seldom possible to experiment on large organized systems as a whole in their natural environments.

These results in an apparent dilemma: to gain understanding of complex systems experimentation seems to be necessary, but it cannot usually be carried out. This difficulty is solved by the use of models, representations of the system under study. Provided the model is good, experiments (called "simulations") can be conducted on it, or other methods can be used to obtain useful results.

Phases of operations research

To formulate an operations research problem, a suitable measure of performance must be devised, various possible courses of action defined (that is, controlled variables and the constraints upon them), and relevant uncontrolled variables identified. To devise a measure of performance, objectives are identified and defined, and then quantified.

If objectives cannot be quantified or expressed in rigorous (usually mathematical) terms, most operations research techniques cannot be applied. For example, a business manager may have the acquisitive objective of introducing a new product and making it profitable within one year.

125

The identified objective is profit in one year, which is defined as receipts less costs, and would probably be quantified in terms of sales. In the real world, conditions may change with time. Thus, though a given objective is identified at the beginning of the period, change and reformulation are frequently necessary.

Detailed knowledge of how the system under study actually operates and of its environment is essential.

Such knowledge is normally acquired through an analysis of the system, a four-step process that involves:

- Determining whose needs or desires the organization tries to satisfy;
- How these are communicated to the organization;
- How information on needs and desires penetrates the organization; and
- What action is taken, how it is controlled, and what the time and resource requirements of these actions are.

This information can usually be represented graphically in a flowchart, which enables researchers to identify the variables that affect system performance.

Once the objectives, the decision makers, their courses of action, and the uncontrolled variables have been identified and defined, a measure of performance can be developed and selection can be made of a quantitative function of this measure to be used as a criterion for the best solution.

The type of decision criterion that is appropriate to a problem depends on the state of knowledge regarding possible outcomes. Certainty describes a situation in which each course of action is believed to result in one particular outcome.

Risk is a situation in which, for each course of action, alternative outcomes are possible, the probabilities of which are known or can be estimated. Uncertainty describes a situation in which, for each course of action, probabilities cannot be assigned to the possible outcomes.

In risk situations, which are the most common in practice, the objective normally is to maximize expected (long-run average) net gain or gross gain for specified costs, or to minimize costs for specified benefits. A business, for example, seeks to maximize expected profits or minimize expected costs.

Other objectives, not necessarily related, may be sought; for example, an economic planner may wish to maintain full employment without inflation; or different groups within an organization may have to compromise their differing objectives, as when an army and a navy, for example, must cooperate in matters of defence.

In approaching uncertain situations one may attempt either to maximize the minimum gain or minimize the

127

maximum loss that results from a choice; this is the "minimax" approach.

Alternatively, one may weigh the possible outcomes to reflect one's optimism or pessimism and then apply the minimax principle. A third approach, "minimax regret," attempts to minimize the maximum deviation from the outcome that would have been selected if a state of certainty had existed before the choice had been made.

Each identified variable should be defined in terms of the conditions under which, and research operations by which, questions concerning its value ought to be answered; this includes identifying the scale used in measuring the variable.

Model construction

A model is a simplified representation of the real world and, as such, includes only those variables relevant to the problem at hand. A model of freely falling bodies, for example, does not refer to the colour, texture, or shape of the body involved.

Furthermore, a model may not include all relevant variables because a small percentage of these may account for most of the phenomenon to be explained.

Many of the simplifications used produce some error in predictions derived from the model, but these can often be kept small compared to the magnitude of the improvement in operations that can be extracted from them.

Most operations research models are symbolic models because symbols represent properties of the system. The earliest models were physical representations such as model ships, airplanes, tow tanks, and wind tunnels.

Physical models are usually fairly easy to construct, but only for relatively simple objects or systems, and are usually difficult to change.

The next step beyond the physical model is the graph, easier to construct and manipulate but more abstract. Since graphic representation of more than three variables is difficult, symbolic models came into use.

There is no limit to the number of variables that can be included in a symbolic model, and such models are easier to construct and manipulate than physical models.

Symbolic models are completely abstract. When the symbols in a model are defined, the model is given content or meaning.

This has important consequences. Symbolic models of systems of very different content often reveal similar structure. Hence, most systems and problems arising in them can be fruitfully classified in terms of relatively few structures.

Furthermore, since methods of extracting solutions from models depend only on their structure, some methods can be used to solve a wide variety of problems from a contextual point of view.

Finally, a system that has the same structure as another, however different the two may be in content, can be used as a model of the other. Such a model is called an analogue. By use of such models much of what is known about the first system can be applied to the second.

Despite the obvious advantages of symbolic models there are many cases in which physical models are still useful, as in testing physical structures and mechanisms; the same is true for graphic models. Physical and graphic models are frequently used in the preliminary phases of constructing symbolic models of systems.

Operations research models represent the causal relationship between the controlled and uncontrolled variables and system performance; they must therefore be explanatory, not merely descriptive. Only explanatory models can provide the requisite means to manipulate the system to produce desired changes in performance.

Operations research analysis is directed toward establishing cause-and-effect relations. Though experiments with actual operations of all or part of a system are often useful, these are not the only way to analyze cause and effect.

There are four patterns of model construction, only two of which involve experimentation:

130

- Inspection, use of analogues,
- Operational analysis and operational experiments.

They are considered here in order of increasing complexity.

In some cases the system and its problem are relatively simple and can be grasped either by inspection or from discussion with persons familiar with it. In general, only low-level and repetitive operating problems, those in which human behaviour plays a minor role can be so treated.

When the researcher finds it difficult to represent the structure of a system symbolically, it is sometimes possible to establish a similarity, if not an identity, with another system whose structure is better known and easier to manipulate. It may then be possible to use either the analogous system itself or a symbolic model of it as a model of the problem system.

For example, an equation derived from the kinetic theory of gases has been used as a model of the movement of trains between two classification yards.

Hydraulic analogues of economies and electronic analogues of automotive traffic have been constructed with which experimentation could be carried out to determine the effects of manipulation of controllable variables. Thus, analogues may be constructed as well as found in existing systems.

In some cases analysis of actual operations of a system may reveal its causal structure. Data on operations are

131

analyzed to yield an explanatory hypothesis, which is tested by analysis of operating data. Such testing may lead to revision of the hypothesis. The cycle is continued until a satisfactory explanatory model is developed.

For example, an analysis of the cars stopping at urban automotive service stations located at intersections of two streets revealed that almost all came from four of the 16 possible routes through the intersection (four ways of entering times four ways of leaving).

Examination of the percentage of cars in each route that stopped for service suggested that this percentage was related to the amount of time lost by stopping. Data were then collected on time lost by cars in each route.

This revealed a close inverse relationship between the percentage stopping and time lost. But the relationship was not linear; that is, the increases in one were not proportional to increases in the other. It was then found that perceived lost time exceeded actual lost time, and the relationship between the percentage of cars stopping and perceived lost time was close and linear.

The hypothesis was systematically tested and verified and a model constructed that related the number of cars stopping at service stations to the amount of traffic in each route through its intersection and to characteristics of the station that affect the time required to get service.

132

In situations where it is not possible to isolate the effects of individual variables by analysis of operating data, it may be necessary to resort to operational experiments to determine which variables are relevant and how they affect system performance.

Such is the case, for example, in attempts to quantify the effects of advertising (amount, timing, and media used) upon sales of a consumer product.

Advertising by the producer is only one of many controlled and uncontrolled variables affecting sales. Hence, in many cases its effect can only be isolated and measured by controlled experiments in the field.

The same is true in determining how the size, shape, weight, and price of a food product affect its sales. In this case laboratory experiments on samples of consumers can be used in preliminary stages, but field experiments are eventually necessary.

Experiments do not yield explanatory theories, however. They can only be used to test explanatory hypotheses formulated before designing the experiment and to suggest additional hypotheses to be tested.

It is sometimes necessary to modify an otherwise acceptable model because it is not possible or practical to find the numerical values of the variables that appear in it.

For example, a model to be used in guiding the selection of research projects may contain such

133

variables as "the probability of success of the project," "expected cost of the project," and its "expected yield." But none of these may be calculable with any reliability.

Models not only assist in solving problems but also are useful in formulating them; that is, models can be used as guides to explore the structure of a problem and to reveal possible courses of action that might otherwise be missed.

In many cases the course of action revealed by such application of a model is so obviously superior to previously considered possibilities that justification of its choice is hardly required.

In some cases the model of a problem may be either too complicated or too large to solve. It is frequently possible to divide the model into individually solvable parts and to take the output of one model as an input to another. Since the models are likely to be interdependent, several repetitions of this process may be necessary.

Deriving solutions from models

Procedures

Procedures for deriving solutions from models are either deductive or inductive. With deduction one moves directly from the model to a solution in either symbolic or numerical form. Such procedures are supplied by mathematics; for example, the calculus. An explicit analytical procedure for finding the solution is called an algorithm.

Even if a model cannot be solved, and many are too complex for solution, it can be used to compare alternative solutions. It is sometimes possible to conduct a sequence of comparisons, each suggested by the previous one and each likely to contain a better alternative than was contained in any previous comparison. Such a solution-seeking procedure is called heuristic.

Inductive procedures involve trying and comparing different values of the controlled variables. Such procedures are said to be iterative (repetitive) if they proceed through successively improved solutions until either an optimal solution is reached or further calculation cannot be justified.

A rational basis for terminating such a process—known as "stopping rules"—involves the determination of the point at which the expected

135

improvement of the solution on the next trial is less than the cost of the trial.

Such well-known algorithms as linear, nonlinear, and dynamic programming are iterative procedures based on mathematical theory. Simulation and experimental optimization are iterative procedures based primarily on statistics.

Testing the model and the solution

A model may be deficient because it includes irrelevant variables, excludes relevant variables, contains inaccurately evaluated variables, is incorrectly structured, or contains incorrectly formulated constraints. Tests for deficiencies of a model are statistical in nature; their use requires knowledge of sampling and estimation theory, experimental designs, and the theory of hypothesis testing.

Sampling-estimation theory is concerned with selecting a sample of items from a large group and using their observed properties to characterize the group as a whole. To save time and money, the sample taken is as small as possible. Several theories of sampling design and estimation are available, each yielding estimates with different properties.

The structure of a model consists of a function relating the measure of performance to the controlled and uncontrolled variables; for example, a business may attempt to show the functional relationship between

136

profit levels (the measure of performance) and controlled variables (prices, amount spent on advertising) and uncontrolled variables (economic conditions, competition). In order to test the model, values of the measure of performance computed from the model are compared with actual values under different sets of conditions. If there is a significant difference between these values, or if the variability of these differences is large, the model requires repair.

Such tests do not use data that have been used in constructing the model, because to do so would determine how well the model fits performance data from which it has been derived, not how well it predicts performance.

The solution derived from a model is tested to find whether it yields better performance than some alternative, usually the one in current use. The test may be prospective, against future performance, or retrospective, comparing solutions that would have been obtained had the model been used in the past with what actually did happen.

If neither prospective nor retrospective testing is feasible, it may be possible to evaluate the solution by "sensitivity analysis," a measurement of the extent to which estimates used in the solution would have to be in error before the proposed solution performs less satisfactorily than the alternative decision procedure.

The cost of implementing a solution should be subtracted from the gain expected from applying it, thus obtaining an estimate of net improvement. Where errors or inefficiencies in applying the solution are possible, these should also be taken into account in estimating the net improvement.

Implementing and controlling the solution

The acceptance of a recommended solution by the responsible manager depends on the extent to which he believes the solution to be superior to alternatives. This in turn depends on his faith in the researchers involved and their methods. Hence, participation by managers in the research process is essential for success.

Operations researchers are normally expected to oversee implementation of an accepted solution. This provides them with an ultimate test of their work and an opportunity to make adjustments if any deficiencies should appear in application. The operations research team prepares detailed instructions for those who will carry out the solution and trains them in following these instructions.

The cooperation of those who carry out the solution and those who will be affected by it should be sought in the course of the research process, not after everything is done. Implementation plans and schedules are pre-tested and deficiencies corrected. Actual performance of the solution is compared with expectations and, where divergence is significant, the reasons for it are determined and appropriate adjustments made.

138

The solution may fail to yield expected performance for one or a combination of reasons: the model may be wrongly constructed or used; the data used in making the model may be incorrect; the solution may be incorrectly carried out; the system or its environment may have changed in unexpected ways after the solution was applied. Corrective action is required in each case.

Controlling a solution requires deciding what constitutes a significant deviation in performance from expectations; determining the frequency of control checks, the size and type of sample of observations to be made, and the types of analyses of the resulting data that should be carried out; and taking appropriate corrective action. The second step should be designed to minimize the sum of the costs of carrying out the control procedures and the errors that might be involved.

Since most models involve a variety of assumptions, these are checked systematically. Such checking requires explicit formulation of the assumptions made during construction of the model. Effective controls not only make possible but often lead to better understanding of the dynamics of the system involved. Through controls the problem-solving system of which operations research is a part learns from its own experience and adapts more effectively to changing conditions.

Computers and operations research simulation

Industrial production systems

Computers have had a dramatic impact on the management of industrial production systems and the fields of operations research and industrial engineering.

The speed and data-handling capabilities of computers allow engineers and scientists to build larger, more realistic models of organized systems and to get meaningful solutions to those models through the use of simulation techniques.

Simulation consists of calculating the performance of a system by evaluating a model of it for randomly selected values of variables contained within it. Most simulation in operations research is concerned with "stochastic" variables; that is, variables whose values change randomly within some probability distribution over time.

The random sampling employed in simulation requires either a supply of random numbers or a procedure for generating them. It also requires a way of converting these numbers into the distribution of the relevant variable, a way of sampling these values, and a way of evaluating the resulting performance.

140

A simulation in which decision making is performed by one or more real decision makers is called "operational gaming." Such simulations are commonly used in the study of interactions of decision makers as in competitive situations. Military gaming has long been used as a training device, but only relatively recently has it been used for research purposes. There is still considerable difficulty, however, in drawing inferences from operational games to the real world.

Experimental optimization is a means of experimenting on a system so as to find the best solution to a problem within it. Such experiments, conducted either simultaneously or sequentially, may be designed in various ways, no one of which is best in all situations.

Decision analysis and support

Since their widespread introduction in business and government organizations in the 1950s, the primary applications of computers have been in the areas of record keeping, bookkeeping, and transaction processing.

These applications, commonly called data processing, automate the flow of paperwork, account for business transactions (such as order processing and inventory and shipping activities), and maintain orderly and accurate records. Although data processing is vital to most organisations, most of the work involved in the design of such systems does not require the methods of operations research.

141

In the 1960s, when computers were applied to the routine decision-making problems of managers, management information systems (MIS) emerged. These systems use the raw (usually historical) data from data-processing systems to prepare management summaries, to chart information on trends and cycles, and to monitor actual performance against plans or budgets.

More recently, decision support systems (DSS) have been developed to project and predict the results of decisions before they are made. These projections permit managers and analysts to evaluate the possible consequences of decisions and to try several alternatives on paper before committing valuable resources to actual programs.

The development of management information systems and decision support systems brought operations researchers and industrial engineers to the forefront of business planning.

These computer-based systems require knowledge of an organization and its activities in addition to technical skills in computer programming and data handling. The key issues in MIS or DSS include how a system will be modelled, how the model of the system will be handled by the computer, what data will be used, how far into the future trends will be extrapolated, and so on. In much of this work, as well as in more traditional operations research modelling, simulation techniques have proved invaluable.

New software tools for decision making

Growth of personal computers

The explosive growth of personal computers in business organizations in the early 1980s spawned a parallel growth in software to assist in decision making.

These tools include spreadsheet programs for analyzing complex problems with trails that have different sets of data, data base management programs that permit the orderly maintenance and manipulation of vast amounts of information, and graphics programs that quickly and easily prepare professional-looking displays of data.

Business programs (software) like these once cost tens of thousands of dollars; now they are widely available, may be used on relatively inexpensive hardware, are easy to use without learning a programming language, and are powerful enough to handle sophisticated, practical business problems.

The availability of spreadsheet, data base, and graphics programs on personal computers has also greatly aided industrial engineers and operations researchers whose work involves the construction, solution, and testing of models.

Easy-to-use software that does not require extensive programming knowledge permits faster, more cost-effective model building and is also helpful in communicating the results of analysis to management. Indeed, many managers now have a computer on their desk and work with spreadsheets and other programs as a routine part of their managerial duties.

Models and applications

Many operational problems of organized systems have common structures. The most common types of structure have been identified as prototype problems, and extensive work has been done on modelling and solving them.

Though all the problems with similar structures do not have the same model, those that apply to them may have a common mathematical structure and hence may be solvable by one procedure. Some real problems consist of combinations of smaller problems, some or all of which fall into different prototypes.

In general, prototype models are the largest that can be solved in one step. Hence, large problems that consist of combinations of prototype problems usually must be broken down into solvable units; the overall model used is an aggregation of prototype and possibly other models.

Resource allocation

Allocation problems involve the distribution of resources among competing alternatives in order to minimize total costs or maximize total return.

Such problems have the following components:

- A set of resources available in given amounts;
- A set of jobs to be done, each consuming a specified amount of resources; and
- A set of costs or returns for each job and resource.

The problem is to determine how much of each resource to allocate to each job.

If more resources are available than needed, the solution should indicate which resources are not to be used, taking associated costs into account.

Similarly, if there are more jobs than can be done with available resources, the solution should indicate which jobs are not to be done, again taking into account the associated costs.

If each job requires exactly one resource (*e.g.,* one person) and each resource can be used on only one job, the resulting problem is one of assignment. If resources are divisible, and if both jobs and resources are expressed in units on the same scale, it is termed a transportation or distribution problem. If jobs and resources are not expressed in the same units, it is a general allocation problem.

145

An assignment problem may consist of assigning workers to offices or jobs, trucks to delivery routes, drivers to trucks, or classes to rooms. A typical transportation problem involves distribution of empty railroad freight cars where needed or the assignment of orders to factories for production.

The general allocation problem may consist of determining which machines should be employed to make a given product or what set of products should be manufactured in a plant during a particular period.

In allocation problems the unit costs or returns may be either independent or interdependent; for example, the return from investing a dollar in selling effort may depend on the amount spent on advertising.

If the allocations made in one period affect those in subsequent periods, the problem is said to be dynamic, and time must be considered in its solution.

Linear programming

Linear programming (LP) refers to a family of mathematical optimization techniques that have proved effective in solving resource allocation problems, particularly those found in industrial production systems.

Linear programming methods are algebraic techniques based on a series of equations or inequalities that limit a problem and are used to optimize a mathematical expression called an objective function.

The objective function and the constraints placed upon the problem must be deterministic and able to be expressed in linear form.

These restrictions limit the number of problems that can be handled directly, but since the introduction of linear programming in the late 1940s, much progress has been made to adapt the method to more complex problems.

Since linear programming is probably the most widely used mathematical optimization technique, numerous computer programs are available for solving LP problems.

For example, LP techniques are now used routinely for such problems as oil and chemical refinery blending, choosing vendors or suppliers for large, multi-plant manufacturing corporations, determining shipping routes and schedules, and managing and maintaining truck fleets.

147

Inventory control

Stocks holding

Inventories include raw materials, component parts, work in process, finished goods, packing and packaging materials, and general supplies. The control of inventories, vital to the financial strength of a firm, in general involves deciding at what points in the production system stocks shall be held and what their form and size are to be.

As some unit costs increase with inventory size— including storage, obsolescence, deterioration, insurance, investment—and other unit costs decrease with inventory size—including setup or preparation costs, delays because of shortages, and so forth—a good part of inventory management consists of determining optimal purchase or production lot sizes and base stock levels that will balance the opposing cost influences.

Another part of the general inventory problem is deciding the levels (reorder points) at which orders for replenishment of inventories are to be initiated.

Inventory control is concerned with two questions: when to replenish the store and by how much. There are two main control systems. The two-bin system (sometimes called the min-max system) involves the use of two bins, either physically or on paper. The first bin is intended for supplying current demand and the second for satisfying demand during the replenishment period.

When the stock in the first bin is depleted, an order for a given quantity is generated. The reorder-cycle system, or cyclical-review system, consists of ordering at fixed regular intervals. Various combinations of these systems can be used in the construction of an inventory-control procedure.

A pure two-bin system, for example, can be modified to require cyclical instead of continuous review of stock, with orders being generated only when the stock falls below a specific level. Similarly, a pure reorder-cycle system can be modified to allow orders to be generated if the stock falls below the reorder level between the cyclical reviews.

In yet another variation, the reorder quantity in the reorder-cycle system is made to depend on the stock level at the review period or the need to order other products or materials at the same time or both.

Inventory problems

The classic inventory problem involves determining how much of a resource to acquire, either by purchasing or producing it, and whether or when to acquire it to minimize the sum of the costs that increase with the size of inventory and those that decrease with increases in inventory.

Costs of the first type include the cost of the capital invested in inventory, handling, storage, insurance, taxes, depreciation, deterioration, and obsolescence. Costs that decrease as inventory increases include shortage costs (arising from lost sales), production setup costs, and the purchase price or direct production costs. Setup costs include the cost of placing a purchase order or starting a production run.

If large quantities are ordered, inventories increase but the frequency of ordering decreases, hence setup costs decrease. In general, the larger the quantity ordered the lower the unit purchase price because of quantity discounts and the lower production cost per unit resulting from the greater efficiency of long production runs. Other relevant variables include demand for the resource and the time between placing and filling orders.

Inventory problems arise in a wide variety of contexts; for example, determining quantities of goods to be purchased or produced, how many people to hire or train, how large a new production or retailing facility should be or how many should be provided, and how much fluid (operating) capital to keep available.

Inventory models for single items are well developed and are normally solved with calculus. When the order quantities for many items are interdependent (as, for example, when there is limited storage space or production time) the problem is more difficult.

Some of the larger problems can be solved by breaking them into interacting inventory and allocation problems. In very large problems simulation can be used to test various relevant decision rules.

Japanese approaches

In the 1970s several Japanese firms, led by the Toyota Motor Corporation, developed radically different approaches to the management of inventories. Coined the "just-in-time" approach, the basic element of the new systems was the dramatic reduction of inventories throughout the total production system.

By relying on careful scheduling and the coordination of supplies, the Japanese ensured that parts and supplies were available in the right quantity, with proper quality, at the exact time they were needed in the manufacturing or assembly process.

Two things made just-in-time work—a dogged attention to quality at all levels of the total system obviated the need for parts inventories to cover defectives found in the manufacturing process, and a close coordination of information and plans with suppliers and vendors permitted them to align their schedules and shipments with the last-minute needs of the manufacturer.

Elements of the just-in-time approach now have been adopted by numerous companies in the United States and Europe, although many cannot use the system to

151

its fullest extent because their supplier networks are larger and more widely dispersed than in Japan.

A second Japanese technique, called *kanban* ("card"), also permits Japanese firms to schedule production and manage inventories more effectively. In the *kanban* system, cards or tickets are attached to batches, racks, or pallet loads of parts in the manufacturing process.

When a batch is depleted in the assembly process, its *kanban* is returned to the manufacturing department and another batch is shipped immediately. Since the total number of parts or batches in the system is held constant, the coordination, scheduling, and control of the inventory is greatly simplified.

Replacement and maintenance

Replacement problems involve items that degenerate with use or with the passage of time and those that fail after a certain amount of use or time. Items that deteriorate are likely to be large and costly (*e.g.,* machine tools, trucks, ships, and home appliances).

Non-deteriorating items tend to be small and relatively inexpensive (*e.g.,* light bulbs, vacuum tubes, ink cartridges). The longer a deteriorating item is operated the more maintenance it requires to maintain efficiency.

Furthermore, the longer such an item is kept the less is its resale value and the more likely it is to be made obsolete by new equipment. If the item is replaced frequently, however, investment costs increase. Thus the problem is to determine when to replace such items and how much maintenance (particularly preventive) to perform so that the sum of the operating, maintenance, and investment costs is minimized.

In the case of non-deteriorating items the problem involves determining whether to replace them as a group or to replace individuals as they fail. Though group replacement is wasteful, labour cost of replacements is greater when done singly; for example, the light bulbs in a large subway system may be replaced in groups to save labour.

Replacement problems that involve minimizing the costs of items, failures, and the replacement labour are solvable either by numerical analysis or simulation.

The "items" involved in replacement problems may be people. If so, maintenance can be interpreted as training or improvements in salary, status, or fringe benefits. Failure can be interpreted as departure and investment as recruiting, hiring, and initial training costs.

There are many additional complexities in such cases; for example, the effect of one person's resigning or being promoted on the behaviour of others. Such controllable aspects of the environment as location of work and working hours can have a considerable effect on productivity and failure rates.

153

In problems of this type, the inputs of the behavioral sciences are particularly useful.

Queuing

A queue is a waiting line, and queuing involves dealing with items or people in sequence. Thus, a queuing problem consists either of determining what facilities to provide or scheduling the use of them.

The cost of providing service and the waiting time of users are minimized. Examples of such problems include determining the number of checkout counters to provide at a supermarket, runways at an airport, parking spaces at a shopping centre, or tellers in a bank.

Many maintenance problems can be treated as queuing problems; items requiring repair are like users of a service. Some inventory problems may also be formulated as queuing problems in which orders are like users and stocks are like service facilities.

Job shop sequencing

In queuing problems, the order in which users waiting for service are served is always specified. Selection of that order so as to minimize some function of the time to perform all the tasks is a sequencing problem. The performance measure may account for total elapsed time, total tardiness in meeting deadlines or due dates, and the cost of in-process inventories. The most common context for sequencing problems is a batch, or job shop, production facility that processes many different products with many combinations of machines. In this context account may have to be taken of such factors as overlapping service.

That is, if a customer consists of a number of items to be taken through several steps of a process, the first items completing the initial step may start on the second step before the last one finishes the first, transportation time between service facilities, correction of service breakdowns, facility breakdowns, and material shortages.

Manufacturing progress function

Because of the enormous complexity of a typical mass production line and the almost infinite number of changes that can be made and alternatives that can be pursued, a body of quantitative theory of mass production manufacturing systems has not yet been developed.

The volume of available observational data is, however, growing, and qualitative facts are emerging that may eventually serve as a basis for quantitative theory. An example is the "manufacturing progress function." This was first recognized in the airframe industry.

Early manufacturers of aircraft observed that as they produced increasing numbers of a given model of airplane, their manufacturing costs decreased in a predictable fashion, declining steeply at first, and then continuing to decline at a lower rate. When an actual cost graph is drawn on double logarithmic paper plotting the logarithm of the cost per unit as a function of the logarithm of the total number of units produced results in data points that almost form a straight line.

Over the years similar relationships have been found for many products manufactured by mass production techniques. The slope of the straight line varies from product to product. For a given class of products and a given type of production technology, however, the slope appears remarkably constant. Manufacturing progress functions can be of great value to the manufacturer, serving as a useful tool in estimating future costs. Furthermore, the failure of costs to follow a well-established progress function may be a sign that more attention should be given to the operation in order to bring its cost performance in line with expectation.

Though manufacturing progress functions are sometimes called "learning curves," they reflect much more than the improved training of the manufacturing operators. Improved operator skill is important in the start-up of production, but the major portion of the long-term cost improvement is contributed by improvements in product design, machinery, and the overall engineering planning of the production sequence.

Network routing

Nodes connectivity

A network may be defined by a set of points, or "nodes," that are connected by lines, or "links." A way of going from one node (the "origin") to another (the "destination") is called a "route" or "path." Links, which may be one-way or two-way, are usually characterized by the time, cost, or distance required to traverse them. The time or cost of travelling in different directions on the same link may differ.

A network routing problem consists of finding an optimum route between two or more nodes in relation to total time, cost, or distance. Various constraints may exist, such as a prohibition on returning to a node already visited or a stipulation of passing through every node only once.

Network routing problems commonly arise in communication and transportation systems. Delays that occur at the nodes (*e.g.*, railroad classification yards or telephone switchboards) may be a function of the loads placed on them and their capacities. Breakdowns may occur in either links or nodes.

Much studied is the "travelling salesman problem," which consists of starting a route from a designated node that goes through each node (*e.g.*, city) only once and returns to the origin in the least time, cost, or distance.

This problem arises in selecting an order for processing a set of production jobs when the cost of setting up each job depends on which job has preceded it. In this case the jobs can be thought of as nodes, each of which is connected to all of the others, with setup costs as the analogue of distances between them.

The order that yields the least total setup cost is therefore equivalent to a solution to the travelling salesman problem. The complexity of the calculations is such that even with the use of computers it is very costly to handle more than 20 nodes. Less costly approximating procedures are available, however.

More typical routing problems involve getting from one place to another in the least time, cost, or distance. Both graphic and analytic procedures are available for finding such routes.

Competitive problems

Competitive problems deal with choice in interactive situations where the outcome of one decision maker's choice depends on the choice, either helpful or harmful, of one or more others. Examples of these are war, marketing, and bidding for contracts.

Competitive problems are classifiable as certain, risky, or uncertain, depending on the state of a decision maker's knowledge of his opponent's choices. Under conditions of certainty, it is easy to maximize gain or minimize loss.

Competitive problems of the risk type require the use of statistical analysis for their solution; the most difficult aspect of solving such problems usually lies in estimating the probabilities of the competitor's choices; for example, in bidding for a contract on which competitors and their bids are unknown.

The theory of games was developed to deal with a large class of competitive situations of the uncertainty type in which each participant knows what choices he and each other participant has. There is a well-defined "end state" that terminates the interaction (*e.g.,* win, lose, or draw), and the payoffs associated with each end state are specified in advance and are known to each participant.

In situations in which all the alternatives are open to competition, or some of their outcomes are not known in advance, operational gaming can sometimes be used. The military have long constructed operational games; their use by business is more recent.

Search problems

Search problems involve finding the best way to obtain information needed for a decision. Though every problem contains a search problem in one sense, situations exist in which search itself is the essential

159

process; for example, in auditing accounts, inspection and quality control procedures, in exploration for minerals, in the design of information systems, and in military problems involving the location of such threats as enemy ships, aircraft, mines, and missiles.

Two kinds of error are involved in search: those of observation and those of sampling. Observational errors, in turn, are of two general types: commission, seeing something that is not there; and omission, not seeing something that is there.

In general, as the chance of making one of these errors is decreased, the chance of making the other is increased. Furthermore, if fixed resources are available for search, the larger the sample (and hence the smaller the sampling error), the less resources available per observation (and hence the larger the observational error).

The cost of search is composed of setup or design cost, cost of observations, cost of analyzing the data obtained, and cost of error. The objective is to minimize these costs by manipulating the sample size (amount of observation), the sample design (how the things or places to be observed are selected), and the way of analyzing the data (the inferential procedure).

Almost all branches of statistics provide useful techniques for solving search problems. In search problems that involve the location of physical objects, particularly those that move, physics and some fields of mathematics (*e.g.,* geometry and trigonometry) are also applicable.

A "reversed-search" problem arises when the search procedure is not under control but the object of the search is. Most retailers, for example, cannot control the manner in which customers search for goods in their stores, but they can control the location of the goods.

This type of problem also arises in the design of libraries and information systems, and in laying land and sea mines. These, too, are search problems, and solution techniques described above are applicable to them.

Frontiers of operations research

Operations research is a rapidly developing application of the scientific method to organizational problems. Its growth has consisted of both technical development and enlargement of the class of organized systems and the class of problems to which it is applied.

161

Strategic problems

Tactics and strategy are relative concepts.

The distinction between them depends on three considerations:

(1) Longer the effect of a decision and the less reversible it is, the more strategic it is, the;

(2) Larger the portion of a system that is affected by a decision, the more strategic it is; and

(3) More concerned a decision is with the selection of goals and objectives, as well as the means by which they are to be obtained, the more strategic it is.

Strategy and tactics are separable only in thought, not in action. Every tactical decision involves a strategic choice, no matter how implicit and unconscious it may be. Since the strategic aspects of decisions are usually suppressed, an organization's strategy often emerges as an accidental consequence of its tactical decisions.

Operations research is becoming increasingly concerned with strategic decisions and the development of explicit strategies for organizations so as to improve the quality of their tactical decisions and make even the most immediate and urgent of these contribute to its long-run goals.

162

System design problem

Operations research has traditionally been concerned with finding effective solutions to specific operational problems. It has developed better methods, techniques, and tools for doing so. But operations researchers have found that too many of their solutions are not implemented and, of those that are, too few survive the inclination of organizations to return to familiar ways of doing things.

Therefore, operations researchers have gradually come to realize that their task should not only include solving specific problems but also designing problem-solving and implementation systems that predict and prevent future problems, identify and solve current ones, and implement and maintain these solutions under changing conditions.

Planning problem

Operations researchers have come to realize that most problems do not arise in isolation but are part of an interacting system. The process of seeking simultaneous interrelated solutions to a set of interdependent problems is planning. More and more operations research effort is being devoted to developing a rational methodology of such planning, particularly strategic planning.

163

Most organizations resist changes in their operations or management. The organizational need to find better ways of doing things is often not nearly as great as is the need to maximize use of what it already knows or has.

This is apparent in many underdeveloped countries that, while complaining about the lack of required resources, use what resources they have with considerably less efficiency than do most developed countries.

Operations research, therefore, has been addressing itself more and more to determining how to produce the willingness to change.

Types of organisation

Operations researchers have become increasingly aware of the need to distinguish between different types of organization because their distinguishing features affect how one must go about solving their problems. Two important classifications exist, the first of which is homogeneous–heterogeneous.

Homogeneous organizations are those in which membership involves serving the objectives of the whole (*e.g.,* a corporation or military unit), while heterogeneous organizations are those whose principal objective it is to serve the objectives of its members (*e.g.,* a university or city). The second classification is unimodal–multimodal.

164

Uni-modal organizations are hierarchical organizations with a single decision-making authority that can resolve differences between any lower level decision makers. Multi-modal organizations have no such authority but have diffused decision making and hence require agreement among the several decision makers in order to reach conclusions. Since current skills in operations research are largely restricted to homogeneous uni-modal organizations, attempts are under way to develop methodologies adequate for improving the other three types of organization.

In order to solve any of the preceding problems more effectively, operations research requires a better understanding of human behaviour, individual and collective, than is currently available. Furthermore, what understanding the behavioural sciences claim to provide is seldom available in a form that lends itself to symbolic representation and hence to operations research methodology.

Operations researchers, therefore, are increasingly working with behavioural scientists to develop behavioural theories that are expressible in a more usable form. As the scope of problems to which operations research addresses itself increases, it becomes more apparent that the number of disciplines and inter-disciplines that have an important contribution to make to their solution also increases.

An attempt to provide such a higher order integration of scientific activity is being made in the management sciences.

165

Cloud computing

Running and storing data

Cloud computing is the method for running application software and storing related data in central computer systems and providing customers or other users access to them through the Internet.

Early development

The origin of the expression *cloud computing* is obscure, but it appears to derive from the practice of using drawings of stylized clouds to denote networks in diagrams of computing and communications systems.

The term came into popular use in 2008, though the practice of providing remote access to computing functions through networks dates back to the mainframe time-sharing systems of the 1960s and 1970s.

In his 1966 book *The Challenge of the Computer Utility*, the Canadian electrical engineer Douglas F. Parkhill predicted that the computer industry would come to resemble a public utility "in which many remotely located users are connected via communication links to a central computing facility."

For decades, efforts to create large-scale computer utilities were frustrated by constraints on the capacity

166

of telecommunications networks such as the telephone system. It was cheaper and easier for companies and other organizations to store data and run applications on private computing systems maintained within their own facilities.

The constraints on network capacity began to be removed in the 1990s when telecommunications companies invested in high-capacity fibre-optic networks in response to the rapidly growing use of the Internet as a shared network for exchanging information. In the late 1990s, a number of companies, called application service providers (ASPs), were founded to supply computer applications to companies over the Internet.

Most of the early ASPs failed, but their model of supplying applications remotely became popular a decade later, when it was renamed cloud computing.

Cloud services and major providers

Cloud computing encompasses a number of different services. One set of services, sometimes called software as a service (SaaS), involves the supply of a discrete application to outside users. The application can be geared either to business users (such as an accounting application) or to consumers (such as an application for storing and sharing personal photographs).

Another set of services, variously called utility computing, grid computing, and hardware as a service

167

(HaaS), involves the provision of computer processing and data storage to outside users, who are able to run their own applications and store their own data on the remote system. A third set of services, sometimes called platform as a service (PaaS), involves the supply of remote computing capacity along with a set of software-development tools for use by outside software programmers.

Early pioneers of cloud computing include Salesforce.com, which supplies a popular business application for managing sales and marketing efforts; Google, Inc., which in addition to its search engine supplies an array of applications, known as Google Apps, to consumers and businesses; and Amazon Web Services, a division of online retailer Amazon.com, which offers access to its computing system to Web-site developers and other companies and individuals.

Cloud computing also underpins popular social networks and other online media sites such as Facebook, MySpace, and Twitter. Traditional software companies, including Microsoft Corporation, Apple Inc., Intuit Inc., and Oracle Corporation, have also introduced cloud applications.

Cloud-computing companies either charge users for their services, through subscriptions and usage fees, or provide free access to the services and charge companies for placing advertisements in the services. Because the profitability of cloud services tends to be much lower than the profitability of selling or licensing hardware components and software programs, it is viewed as a potential threat to the businesses of many traditional computing companies.

Data centres and privacy

Construction of the large data centres that run cloud-computing services often requires investments of hundreds of millions of dollars. The centres typically contain thousands of server computers networked together into parallel-processing or grid-computing systems.

The centres also often employ sophisticated virtualization technologies, which allow computer systems to be divided into many virtual machines that can be rented temporarily to customers. Because of their intensive use of electricity, the centres are often located near hydroelectric dams or other sources of cheap and plentiful electric power.

Because cloud computing involves the storage of often sensitive personal or commercial information in central database systems run by third parties, it raises concerns about data privacy and security as well as the transmission of data across national boundaries.

It also stirs fears about the eventual creation of data monopolies or oligopolies. Some believe that cloud computing will, like other public utilities, come to be heavily regulated by governments.

Twentieth century contributors to computing

Bachman, Charles William

Born Dec. 11, 1924, Manhattan, Kan., U.S.

American computer scientist and winner of the 1973 A.M. Turing Award, the highest honour in computer science, for "his outstanding contributions to database technology."

At the time of Bachman's birth, his father was the head football coach at Kansas Agriculture College in Manhattan, and the family subsequently followed the father's trajectory through head coaching jobs at the University of Florida in Gainseville and Michigan State College (now Michigan State University) in East Lansing.

By January 1943, Bachman had enough credits to graduate with his high school class, so he began courses at Michigan State. By the end of the summer, having graduated with his high school class and finished the first year of course work at Michigan State, Bachman joined the U.S. Army and served in the Pacific theatre during World War II.

Following his discharge from the military in 1946, Bachman returned to Michigan State, where in 1948 he earned a bachelor's degree in mechanical engineering. In 1950 Bachman earned a master's degree in mechanical engineering from the University of Pennsylvania, where he also attended the Wharton School of Business.

On graduation, he worked as an engineer on operations research problems for Dow Chemical Company in Midland, Mich., where in 1957 he was chosen to be the first head of a new data-processing division.

Though Bachman selected a digital computer from IBM for purchase and hired a team of computer programmers and data analysts, Dow backed out of the arrangement in 1960.

In 1961 Bachman joined the General Electric Company in New York City, where he developed one of the first database management systems. When Honeywell Inc. acquired General Electric's computer business in 1970, Bachman went to work in Boston for Honeywell's advanced research group.

In 1981 Bachman moved on to nearby Cullinane Database Systems Inc., where he worked on database design before leaving in 1983 to found his own consulting firm, Bachman Information Systems, Inc. His firm went through several mergers and acquisitions before Bachman turned to freelance consultation. In 1996 Bachman retired to Tucson, Ariz.

Bachman holds more than a dozen U.S. patents in database software and was elected a distinguished fellow of the British Computer Society in 1977.

171

Codd, Edgar Frank

Born Aug. 23, 1923, Portland, Dorset, Eng.

Died April 18, 2003, Williams Island, Fla., U.S.

British-born American computer scientist and mathematician who devised the "relational" data model, which led to the creation of the relational database, a standard method of retrieving and storing computer data.

Codd interrupted his study of mathematics and chemistry at the University of Oxford to become a pilot in the Royal Air Force during World War II. Following graduation in 1948 he moved to the United States, and he later became a U.S. citizen.

Codd joined IBM in 1949 and worked as a mathematical programmer on some of the company's early computers. He invented the technique of multi-tasking, which allows several programs to run at once.

In 1967, after receiving a doctorate in computer science (one of the first degrees for the study of cellular automata) from the University of Michigan, Codd moved to IBM's Research Laboratory in San Jose, Calif.

In 1970 Codd published his seminal paper *A Relational Model of Data for Large Shared Data Banks*, which described a new way of structuring data using ideas from set theory that eliminated the need for knowledge about the internal structure of a database. Although

IBM researchers Donald D. Chamberlin and Raymond F. Boyce developed SEQUEL, later named Structured Query Language (SQL), in the early 1970s, the company was slow to market the relational database system, which only the most advanced computers of the time were capable of running.

Meanwhile, Codd's ideas were put into practice by several new companies founded in or around Silicon Valley, including Oracle Corporation, Informix Corporation, and Sybase Inc., before IBM introduced its SQL/DS in 1981. In 1983 SQL/DS was renamed DB2, and it remained IBM's main database management system (DBMS) into the 21st century.

Codd was honoured for his achievements by the Association of Computing Machinery, the British Computer Society, the National Academy of Engineering, the American Academy of Arts and Sciences, and the Institute of Electrical and Electronics Engineers.

In 1981 Codd received the A.M. Turing Award, the highest honour for computer science.

END

Index

ANDREAS SOFRONIOU

ANDREAS SOFRONIOU

ANDREAS SOFRONIOU

Bibliography

ALL BOOKS LISTED BELOW ARE PUBLISHED BY ANDREAS SOFRONIOU

1. THERAPEUTIC PSYCHOLOGY, ISBN: 978-1-326-34523-5
2. MEDICAL ETHICS THROUGH THE AGES, ISBN: 978-1-4092- 7468-1
3. MEDICAL ETHICS, FROM HIPPOCRATES TO THE 21ST CENTURY ISBN: 978-1-4457-1203-1
4. MISINTERPRETATION OF SIGMUND FREUD, ISBN: 978-1-4467-1659-5
5. JUNG'S PSYCHOTHERAPY: THE PSYCHOLOGICAL & MYTHOLOGICAL METHODS, ISBN: 978-1-4477-4740-6
6. FREUDIAN ANALYSIS & JUNGIAN SYNTHESIS, ISBN: 978-1-4477-5996-6
7. ADLER'S INDIVIDUAL PSYCHOLOGY AND RELATED METHODS, ISBN: 978-1-291-85951-5
8. ADLERIAN INDIVIDUALISM , JUNGIAN SYNTHESIS, FREUDIAN ANALYSIS, ISBN: 978-1-291-85937-9
9. PSYCHOTHERAPY, CONCEPTS OF TREATMENT, ISBN: 978-1-291-50178-0
10. PSYCHOLOGY, CONCEPTS OF BEHAVIOUR, ISBN: 978-1-291-47573-9
11. PHILOSOPHY FOR HUMAN BEHAVIOUR, ISBN: 978-1-291-12707-2
12. SEX, AN EXPLORATION OF SEXUALITY, EROS AND LOVE, ISBN: 978-1-291-56931-5
13. PSYCHOLOGY FROM CONCEPTION TO SENILITY, ISBN: 978-1-4092-7218-2
14. PSYCHOLOGY OF CHILD CULTURE, ISBN: 978-1-4092-7619-7
15. JOYFUL PARENTING, ISBN: 0 9527956 1 2
16. GUIDE TO A JOYFUL PARENTING, ISBN: 0 952 7956 1 2
17. THERAPEUTIC PHILOSOPHY FOR THE INDIVIDUAL AND THE STATE, ISBN: 978-1-4092-7586-2
18. PHILOSOPHIC COUNSELLING FOR PEOPLE AND THEIR GOVERNMENTS, ISBN: 978-1-4092-7400-1
19. CHILD PSYCHOTHERAPY, ISBN: 978-1-326-44169-2
20. HYPNOTHERAPY IN MEDICINE, PSYCHOLOGY, MAGIC, ISBN: 978-1-326-48163-6
21. ART FOR PSYCHOTHERAPY, ISBN: 978-1-326-78959-6
22. SLEEPING AND DREAMING EXPLAINED BY ARTS & SCIENCE, ISBN: ISBN: 978-1-326-81309-3

23. PHILOSOPHY AND POLITICS, ISBN: 978-1-326-33854-1
24. MORAL PHILOSOPHY, FROM SOCRATES TO THE 21ST AEON, ISBN: 978-1-4457-4618-0
25. MORAL PHILOSOPHY, FROM HIPPOCRATES TO THE 21ST AEON, ISBN: 978-1-84753-463-7
26. MORAL PHILOSOPHY, THE ETHICAL APPROACH THROUGH THE AGES, ISBN: 978-1-4092-7703-3
27. MORAL PHILOSOPHY, ISBN: 978-1-4478-5037-3
28. 2011 POLITICS, ORGANISATIONS, PSYCHOANALYSIS, POETRY, ISBN: 978-1-4467-2741-6
29. WISDOM AN ACCUMULATION OF KNOWLEDGE, ISBN: 978-1-326-99692-5
30. MYTHOLOGY LEGENDS FROM AROUND THE GLOBE, ISBN: 978-1-326-98630-8
31. PLATO'S EPISTEMOLOGY, ISBN: 978-1-4716-6584-4
32. ARISTOTLE'S AETIOLOGY, ISBN: 978-1-4716-7861-5
33. MARXISM, SOCIALISM & COMMUNISM, ISBN: 978-1-4716-8236-0
34. MACHIAVELLI'S POLITICS & RELEVANT PHILOSOPHICAL CONCEPTS, ISBN: 978-1-4716-8629-0
35. BRITISH PHILOSOPHERS, 16TH TO 18TH CENTURY, ISBN: 978-1-4717-1072-8
36. ROUSSEAU ON WILL AND MORALITY, ISBN: 978-1-4717-1070-4
37. EPISTEMOLOGY, A SYSTEMATIC OVERVIEW, ISBN: 978-1-326-11380-3
38. HEGEL ON IDEALISM, KNOWLEDGE & REALITY, ISBN: 978-1-4717-0954-8
39. METAPHYSICS FACTS AND FALLACIES, ISBN: 978-1-326-80745-0
40. SOCIAL SCIENCES AND PHILOLOGY, ISBN: 978-1-326-33840-4
41. PHILOLOGY, CONCEPTS OF EUROPEAN LITERATURE, ISBN: 978-1-291-49148-7
42. THREE MILLENNIA OF HELLENIC PHILOLOGY, ISBN: 978-1-291-49799-1
43. CYPRUS, PERMANENT DEPRIVATION OF FREEDOM, ISBN: 978-1-291-50833-8
44. SOCIOLOGY, CONCEPTS OF GROUP BEHAVIOUR, ISBN: 978-1-291-51888-7
45. SOCIAL SCIENCES, CONCEPTS OF BRANCHES AND RELATIONSHIPS ISBN: 978-1-291-52321-8
46. CONCEPTS OF SOCIAL SCIENTISTS AND GREAT THINKERS, ISBN: 978-1-

291-53786-4
47. EMPIRES AND COLONIALISM ISBN: 978-1-326-46761-6
48. CYPRUS, COLONISED BY MOST EMPIRES, ISBN, 978-1-326-47164-4
49. PERICLES, GOLDEN AGE OF ATHENS, ISBN: 978-1-326-47592-5
50. TRIANGLE OF EDUCATION TRAINING EXPERIENCE, ISBN: 978-1- 326-82934-6
51. HARMONY IS LOVE FRIENDSHIP SEX, ISBN: 978-1-326-85687-8
52. INTERNATIONAL HUMAN RIGHTS, ISBN: 978-1-326-87348-6
53. ANALYSIS OF LOGIC AND SANITY, ISBN: ISBN: 978-1-326-90604-7
54. INTERNATIONAL LAW, GLOBAL RELATIONS, WORLD POWERS, ISBN: 978-1-326-92921-3
55. MANAGEMENT SCIENCE AND BUSINESS, ISBN: 978-1-326-45508-8
56. ECONOMICS WORLD HOUSE RULES, ISBN: 978-1-326-96162-6
57. POLITICAL SYSTEMS NORMS AND LAWS, ISBN: 978-1-326-97404-6
58. HISTORY OF SYSTEMS, ENGINEERING, TECHNOLOGY, ISBN: 978-1-326-94420-9
59. INFORMATION TECHNOLOGY AND MANAGEMENT, ISBN: 978-1-326-34496-2
60. I.T. RISK MANAGEMENT, ISBN: 978-1-4467-5653-9
61. SYSTEMS ENGINEERING, ISBN: 978-1-4477-7553-9
62. BUSINESS INFORMATION SYSTEMS, CONCEPTS AND EXAMPLES, ISBN: 978-1-4092-7338-7
63. A GUIDE TO INFORMATION TECHNOLOGY, ISBN: 978-1-4092-7608-1
64. CHANGE MANAGEMENT IN I.T., ISBN: 978-1-4092-7712-5
65. FRONT-END DESIGN AND DEVELOPMENT FOR SYSTEMS APPLICATIONS, ISBN: 978-1-4092-7588-6
66. I.T RISK MANAGEMENT, ISBN: 978-1-4092-7488-9
67. I.T. RISK MANAGEMENT – 2011 EDITION, ISBN: 978-1-4467- 5653-9
68. SIMPLIFIED PROCEDURES FOR I.T. PROJECTS DEVELOPMENT, ISBN: 978-1-4092-7562-6
69. SIGMA METHODOLOGY FOR RISK MANAGEMENT IN SYSTEMS DEVELOPMENT, ISBN: 978-1-4092-7690-6
70. TRADING ON THE INTERNET IN THE YEAR 2000 AND BEYOND, ISBN: 978-1-4092- 7577
71. STRUCTURED SYSTEMS METHODOLOGY, ISBN: 978-1-4477-6610-0

181

72. INFORMATION TECHNOLOGY LOGICAL ANALYSIS, ISBN: 978-1-4717-1688-1
73. I.T. RISKS LOGICAL ANALYSIS, ISBN: 978-1-4717-1957-8
74. LOGICAL ANALYSIS OF I.T. CHANGES, ISBN: 978-1-4717-2288-2
75. LOGICAL ANALYSIS OF SYSTEMS, RISKS , CHANGES, ISBN: 978-1-4717-2294-3
76. COMPUTING, A PRÉCIS ON SYSTEMS, SOFTWARE AND HARDWARE, ISBN: 978-1-2910-5102-5
77. MANAGE THAT I.T. PROJECT, ISBN: 978-1-4717-5304-6
78. CHANGE MANAGEMENT, ISBN: 978-1-4457-6114-5
79. MANAGEMENT OF COMMERCIAL COMPUTING, ISBN: 978-1-4092-7550-3
80. PROGRAMME MANAGEMENT WORKSHOP, ISBN: 978-1-4092-7583-1
81. MANAGEMENT OF I.T. CHANGES, RISKS, WORKSHOPS, EPISTEMOLOGY, ISBN: 978-1-84753-147-6
82. THE PHILOSOPHICAL CONCEPTS OF MANAGEMENT THROUGH THE AGES, ISBN: 978-1-4092- 7554-1
83. MANAGEMENT OF PROJECTS, SYSTEMS, INTERNET, AND RISKS, ISBN: 978-1-4092- 7464-3
84. HOW TO CONSTRUCT YOUR RESUMÊ, ISBN: 978-1-4092-7383-7
85. DEFINE THAT SYSTEM, ISBN: 978-1-291-15094-0
86. INFORMATION TECHNOLOGY WORKSHOP, ISBN: 978-1-291-16440-4
87. CHANGE MANAGEMENT IN SYSTEMS, ISBN: 978-1-4457-1099-0
88. SYSTEMS MANAGEMENT, ISBN: 978-1-4710-4907-1
89. TECHNOLOGY, A STUDY OF MECHANICAL ARTS AND APPLIED SCIENCES, ISBN: 978-1-291-58550-6
90. EXPERT SYSTEMS, KNOWLEDGE ENGINEERING FOR HUMAN REPLICATION, ISBN: 978-1-291- 59509-3
91. ARTIFICIAL INTELLIGENCE AND INFORMATION TECHNOLOGY, ISBN: 978-1-291- 60445-0
92. PROJECT MANAGEMENT PROCEDURES FOR SYSTEMS DEVELOPMENT, ISBN: 978-0-952-72531-2
93. SURFING THE INTERNET, THEN, NOW, LATER. ISBN: 978-1--291-77653-9
94. ANALYTICAL DIAGRAMS FOR I.T. SYSTEMS, ISBN: 978-1-326-05786-2
95. INTEGRATION OF INFORMATION TECHNOLOGY, ISBN: 978-1-312-64303-1
96. TRAINING FOR CHANGES IN I.T. ISBN: 978-1-326-14325-1
97. WORKSHOP FOR PROJECTS MANAGEMENT, ISBN: 978-1-326-16162-0